The

CHRISTMAS

The Best Experts' Advice for a Memorable Season with Stories and Photos of Holiday Magic

Jeanne Bice, Founder, The Quacker Factory
Clothing and Home Decor

Health Communications, Inc.
HCI Books, the Life Issues Publisher
Deerfield Beach, Florida

www.hcibooks.com
www.ultimatehcibooks.com

We would like to acknowledge the writers and photographers who granted us permission to use their material. Copyright credits for interior photographs appear on each photograph and credits for literary work are listed alphabetically by authors' last names. Contact information as supplied by the photographers and writers can be found in the back matter of this book.

The Lineup. Nancy Bechtolt. All rights reserved.

It's a Wrap. Peggy Frezon. All rights reserved. Originally appeared in A Christmas Wonderland (2006 Regal)

Finding Santa Claus. Elisa Korentayer. All rights reserved.

A Song for Santa. Linda O'Connell. All rights reserved.

Christmas in July. Todd Outcalt. All rights reserved.

(Copyright credits continued on page 283)

Library of Congress Cataloging-in-Publication Data
is available through the Library of Congress.

©2008 Health Communications, Inc.

ISBN-13: 978-0-7573-0754-6
ISBN-10: 0-7573-0754-X

Publisher: Health Communications, Inc.
   3201 S.W. 15th Street
   Deerfield Beach, FL 33442-8190

Cover Design: Larissa Hise Henoch
Cover and Interior Photos: ©Fotolia, ©Jupiter Images
Photo Editor: Justin Rotkowitz
Editor: Carol McAdoo Rehme
Interior Design: Lawna Patterson Oldfield
Photo Stylists: Larissa Hise Henoch, Lawna Patterson Oldfield,
         Andrea Perrine Brower, and Alivia Perrine Brower

Contents

Christmas Outside the Box:
Offbeat and Untraditional Celebrations

Glad Tidings of Great Joy:
Heartfelt and Holy Moments

Bah, Humbug! When Christmas Seems
More Blue Than White

Talking Turkey: Holiday Food and Other Fiascos

Yuletide Traditions: Cherished Customs and New Memories for the Making

Must-Know Info or Making Things Merry

Is something "Ultimately" important to you?
Then we want to know about it. . . .

We hope you enjoyed *The Ultimate Christmas*. We are planning many more books in the Ultimate series, each filled with entertaining stories, must-know facts, and captivating photos. We're always looking for talented writers to share slice-of-life true stories, creative photographers to capture images that a story can't tell, as well as top experts to offer their unique insights on a given topic.

For more information on submission guidelines, or to suggest a topic for an upcoming book, please visit the Ultimate website at **www.ultimatehcibooks.com**, or write to: Submission Guidelines, Ultimate Series, HCI Books, 3201 SW 15th St., Deerfield Beach, FL 33442.

For more information about other books by Health Communications, Inc., please visit **www.hcibooks.com**.

Introduction

I've seen Christmas from all angles: As a child growing up in Wisconsin, I counted the days until we could wake up on a likely snow-filled Christmas morning and enjoy our special family breakfast before bursting into the living room to look at the beautifully decorated tree and the presents beneath it. As a wife and mom of two, I won—and lost—my share of "too-tall-tree debates" with my husband. Then as a widowed mom, with no money for rent, let alone presents, I had to find creative ways to make the holidays memorable. Finally, now, as the founder of The Quacker Factory line of clothing and holiday home accessories on QVC television, I try to help other people stage a colorful and festive environment without breaking their budget or breaking a sweat.

Over the years, I've learned that if you mix a little practicality with some creativity and a little Yuletide spirit, you can create a magical holiday season—and the joyful memories and traditions that go with it. I hope to share what I've learned with you in this all-in-one guide to the "ultimate" holiday season.

Throughout this book, you'll read true stories from others about sweet and tender holiday moments, holiday menus gone awry or the turkey that got away, stories of the Christmas blues made brighter by an act of kindness, or the moment someone was reminded of the *true* meaning of the season.

In addition to the stories, which I hope you'll want to share with your family and friends, I've collected essential must-know tips on making your season bright—from finding the perfect tree to eco-friendly decorating ideas and from simple, elegant recipes for entertaining to curbing your kids of the gimmees. And, since life is nothing without a little color, I hope you'll enjoy the glorious photos within the pages.

It is my hope that you and your family have a magical holiday— and carry the Christmas spirit with you all the year through.

Making Spirits Bright: Spreading Good Will and Good Cheer

The Lineup

By Nancy Bechtolt

Christmas Eve day. One-half shopping day left and this was it. Husband Dick and I, son Rick, and his family descended on the city mall with a mixture of excitement and panic, precipitated by the knowledge that visions of sugarplums were due to start dancing in a matter of hours.

Expeditiously finishing my shopping first, I found an empty chair bordering the main walkway through the mall and settled down for an innocent orgy of people watching. One familiar motto caught my eye on a passing sweatshirt: *Practice senseless beauty and random acts of kindness.* I wondered if the wearer or in fact anyone in the mall that day had time for such luxuries. Sounded unlikely.

My attention soon drifted across the procession of shoppers straight into the living room of a Nordic cottage where Santa Claus and an itinerant lapful of radiant believers sat enthroned in an ample maple rocking chair. Behind him a painted fire roared silently in its huge fireplace. Beside him stood a real Christmas tree trimmed with ropes of fake cranberries and popcorn and genuine candy canes.

I was close enough to notice a sheen of perspiration form along the line of Santa's white beard and to hear all of his Christmas questions and most of their answers. A long queue of eager lap replacements and resigned parents wound down the mallway. The line was at least an hour long. That was going to challenge a few Christmas spirits.

Two adjacent families about halfway through the line caught my eye. The first was a mother and a group of little boys about two, four, and five years old. The smallest was corralled in a stroller. That was the good news. The other two were free agents, poking, scuffling, and pushing in the red-blooded way little boys have that amuses onlookers and drives mothers to consider substance abuse.

The children were neatly but modestly dressed in matching red sweatshirts that seemed to have suffered a few indignities from prior owners. But their faces were shiny, their eyes as blue as they were mischievous, and their hair fine, blond, and unruly. Directly behind them stood another family—mother, father, and little girls about five and seven. The girls wore blue velvet dresses, trimmed in lace at the hem and featuring a line of white organdy rosebud buttons. Their long white stockings and black patent Mary Janes had never seen Christmas before. Their long black hair, caught in flowing ponytails, reached almost to their waists. When they squirmed, their parents took turns walking with them to relieve the tedium of the wait.

The line inched forward until the little boys were next. But something was wrong. The boys didn't dash for Santa's lap. Instead, the mother and Santa's linebacker, who guarded access to Santa and a cash register with equal fervor, were in animated conversation.

The mother couldn't believe she had to pay for a set of pictures just so her children could talk to Santa. Wasn't Santa for all children at Christmas? Wasn't every child equal in his sight— even those who didn't have $11.94 for the smallest set of photos? Couldn't they just sit in his lap for a minute, even if she promised not to take a picture with the camera she had brought along?

No, no, no, the linebacker snarled. This was a photo shop in the express business of selling photos. They were not about to overwork Santa for freeloaders. It was too bad she had waited an hour, but the linebacker could take no responsibility for that.

As their voices rose, I realized I was not the only eavesdropper. The father of the blue velvet daughters returned from one of his mini-strolls and, realizing the nature of the controversy, reached into his pocket. He deposited twelve dollars on the cash register.

"This is from one of Santa's plainclothesmen," he grinned. "Now let's get those boys on Santa's lap where they belong."

The mother relaxed. The little boys leaped. Across the aisle, I smiled as tears of pride collected in my eyes.

Santa's plainclothesman was my son.

It's a Wrap

By Peggy Frezon

Mike and I were busy gift-givers—shopping, wrapping, and hiding gifts under the tree. Three-year-old Andy sat and watched as we pulled out colorful paper and carefully tied ribbons and bows. When he begged to help, I handed him the tape dispenser.

He pulled out a sticky length as long as his little arm could stretch. He ripped it off, the tape curling around itself, and secured the paper with the tangled mess. His gifts were covered with more tape than paper.

He sat and watched, too, as we wheeled carts through stores, meticulously selecting a sweater for Uncle Randy and a coloring set for Cousin Crystal.

"What's that?" He pointed at the items I placed in the cart.

"These pretty dishes are for Gramma. And this book is for Kate."

"Me, too," he said.

"No, these are presents we'll give away."

"Me, too," he insisted again. I shrugged and tried to distract him.

On Christmas morning, we all gathered around the tree, ripping paper from packages and exclaiming over new clothes, CDs, and toys. Of course, Andy squealed with delight. He pushed buttons to set off the siren on his new fire truck and gleefully dumped the pieces of his plastic building set all over the floor. Still, several times I noticed him glance anxiously toward the tree.

Finally, he reached beneath the boughs and withdrew a handful of gifts.

"Here Mommy," he said, plopping down in my lap and handing me a present. I recognized the zealously taped wrapping.

"What could this be?" I asked. Mike hadn't mentioned taking him to the store to select anything. I pulled off the holly-green paper and unwrapped a fork. Just like one of the forks in our kitchen drawer. In fact, it was one of the forks from our kitchen drawer. I looked at Andy's little face, glowing with expectancy and pride.

"Why, thank you, Andy. It's just what I wanted!" I laughed and gave him a huge hug. He beamed. He jumped from my lap and handed out the rest of his presents.

Mike worked at his well-taped gift to discover the garage key dangling from its glowing orange chain. "I was wondering where this went," he whispered to me, and then, to Andy, "It's perfect!"

His sister Kate stripped away tape and paper and found a small, well-used blue pony with a rainbow-colored tail. "Thank you, Andy," she played along and gave her brother a big hug.

There were other surprises, too: a deck of cards, a pen, a tape measurer. Andy looked like he'd just given us all a million dollars. And, funny thing was, we all felt like that's what we received.

I don't know when he did it or how he managed to do it in secret. All I know is Andy wanted to be part of Christmas. And he certainly was. He showed us that the spirit of giving really is all wrapped up in the heart—and sometimes with a whole lot of tape.

Finding Santa Claus

By Elisa Korentayer

My experience with Christmas was minimal and not exactly positive.

When I was five years old I learned that, unlike my friends, I was not to expect Santa at my house bearing gifts. To console me, my Jewish mother explained that the big jolly fellow didn't really exist. Santa Claus was a tale spun for little children; the children's parents put the presents under the tree.

Armed with this information, I didn't hesitate to denounce Santa to all the kids on my block. I jeered at their belief in the myth. I stole St. Nick from my young friends simply because they would be getting presents when I would not.

With this childhood faux pas as my sole Christmas memory, I was terrified when my boyfriend Chris invited me to Minnesota for the holidays. I channeled my terror into an obsession with finding perfect gifts for each member of his—as yet unknown— Catholic family. I wanted to get it right.

I scoured New York City, searching in every shop I passed. I spent hours considering what might be right for each individual and days purchasing and then returning gift options. I learned the hard way why people try to complete their shopping before Thanksgiving; I waited in line after line and navigated waves of gift-crazy shoppers in crowds that blew even my city-jaded mind.

I tried to consult with Chris on his family's predilections, but he was no help. He seemed genuinely ignorant of what his family might want, and he tended to err on the side of buying gift cards.

"You don't need to get them anything," he demurred.

But I knew better. I didn't want to seem ungrateful to people who might become important in my life, especially when they were opening their home to me for Christmas.

Only two days before our departure, I finally completed my shopping. I took inventory of the purchases and stuffed a second suitcase with the packages. I even hand-carried a bag of gourmet cookies onto the airplane.

On Christmas Eve, I was as ready as I would ever be. I arrived with Chris to meet his family at St. Henry's Church. They were already there, well-groomed in their Christmas finest. His parents. His sister. Her husband. Their two kids. We filed in as a group.

I was all eyes and ears, taking in the rites of my first Christmas Mass. The choir sang carols as the congregation filled the pews. I was surprised to notice how familiar the songs were. Although I was raised Jewish, it was impossible to avoid the Christmas culture. Seasonal music wafted through stores and from radios. And every year our school choir produced a holiday program full of Christmas songs, with a few Hanukkah tunes tossed in for good measure.

Realization struck: although I was not Catholic, I was American, and therefore Christmas was already partly mine.

After Mass, we joined Chris's family at his parents' house, where we nibbled on hors d'oeuvres and got to know one another. As we sat down to dinner, I could feel the polite smile awkwardly pasted to my face when Chris's father offered grace.

"We give thanks to the God of Abraham, Isaac, and Jacob for what we are about to receive." I was so touched by his sensitivity to my Jewish background that it took me a moment before I could tackle the feast in front of me.

We had ham and turkey and chicken and green beans. We had salads and cheesy potatoes and roast beef. We had carrots and pickles and—the pièce de résistance—cranberry pudding served with decadent sweet gravy known as "hard sauce." It was food heaven.

But that was only the beginning of the celebrations. Chris's family exchanged gifts on Christmas Eve, and I was about to be initiated into their gift-giving tradition. With only my limited experience of Hanukkah and birthday gifts, I couldn't have dreamed up this exercise in Bacchanalian indulgence.

After dinner, we all trooped upstairs to the sitting room where a Christmas tree stood guard over a mountain of presents. I saw the presents I had bought, neatly wrapped and adorned with over-priced bows by underpaid retail workers. To my surprise, I saw countless presents with my name on them.

Chris's young niece and nephew diligently divided the booty into individual piles that they placed at the feet of each adult. Soon, a heap of presents accumulated in front of me. I stared. I don't think I'd ever gotten so many presents at one time.

"Now, we go around the room, taking turns opening one gift at a time," the kids explained the family ritual. They were eager to go first; then I was invited to choose my first gift and open it.

I was paralyzed by indecision. Should I open the red polka-dot box, just the right size for jewelry? Or should I start with the three-foot cube wrapped clumsily by Chris in Santa Claus paper?

"Open that one!" The children decided for me. I reached toward the turquoise and green box they pointed out and got to work.

At first, I tried to open the package neatly. Then I hit the snags of Scotch tape and tore at the wrappings with kamikaze vengeance. Soon, all of us were drowning in crumpled piles of paper, bows, and partly demolished boxes. To the children's amusement, I stuck bows and ribbons on my head.

My smile grew wider and wider till it threatened to split my face in two. I was gleeful. I was giddy. The five-year-old inside me released her disappointment and experienced Santa Claus for herself. At the age of thirty-one, I had finally encountered the jolly old man. He did exist. I found him in the joy of gift-giving and receiving.

It was worth the wait.

A Song for Santa

By Linda O'Connell

L ast year, one week before my preschool's Christmas pageant, the dad who volunteered to play Santa had knee surgery. As the day of the holiday extravaganza drew near, I asked for a volunteer, but no one offered.

Desperate, I cajoled my husband. "Honey, would you please wear the beard and suit for my school pageant?"

On the day of the performance, Bill telephoned my school and I put him on speaker phone. He told the children he was leaving the North Pole en route to St. Louis and he would arrive that evening. The preschoolers cheered and sang him a song: "He's too fat for the chimney, too fat for the chimney. Open the door and let dear Santa come in."

Santa ho-ho-hoed. "Yes, I have been eating a lot of cookies. Tell your teacher to be sure and leave a door open for me tonight."

"We will Santa, we promise! We'll leave the door open," the children shouted in unison.

Before the show began, I escorted Bill to a small back room where the red suit hung on a hook. My high heels clicked like reindeer hooves as I pranced away.

"Wait," he called. "Come back. There's no mirror!"

I had no time to assist him; a crowd of 300 waited. "When you hear us sing 'Jingle Bells' make your grand entrance."

Onstage, I situated the children and welcomed parents and grandparents as they took pictures. What a sight to behold!

During the first song, a girl dressed in red velvet toppled backward from the twelve-inch riser where she sat. She landed in the blue velvet curtain like a piece of felt stuck to a flannel board. Her feet pointed straight up in the air. I interrupted the performance to upright her. "Santa's coming. Santa's coming, hop into bed!" We continued with another song. Little voices rang out and children hopped in place. One mischievous twin got carried away and continued hopping until his pants fell around his ankles. His hands flew to his mouth instead of his trousers and he giggled uncontrollably.

"Pull your pants up!" his mother shouted as she ran onstage. When they hit his ankles a second time, both his mother and I nearly fainted.

A few songs later, a baby made a wild dash from the crowd, climbed like a monkey onto the stage, and shrieked when I carried her off. I felt my blood pressure rise.

After their last song, we all exited the stage. I hurried the students into the hallway to get ready for our grand finale.

The audience oohed and aahed as all sixty children walked out wearing paper antlers and red sparkly noses. Videos zoomed in and cameras flashed as paper noses fell off toddlers when they did the "Reindeer Hokey-Pokey." The auditorium rang with laughter, and the show concluded with a huge round of applause.

In the pause that followed, all eyes swung toward me.

"Santa will arrive as soon as we sing his favorite song," I announced and led the children in "Jingle Bells."

A hush fell over the crowd; eager expectation filled the room; heads swiveled to search the doorway. But Santa did not appear.

I encouraged them to sing again. Still no Santa.

"He's probably parking the sleigh," I stalled. "Why don't you parents sing along?"

Voices rocked the room with a rousing rendition. Both adults and children looked confused when Santa still did not make his grand entrance. My heart palpitated; my deodorant quit working; my mouth went dry.

Then it occurred to me that Santa is hard of hearing.

"Once again, all together now—sing as loud as you can!"

Midway through the chorus, Bill heard his cue. He came barreling out of the back room with his sack slung over his shoulder and his wig a bit cockeyed. "Ho-ho-ho, you children remembered and left the door open for old Santa," he shouted over their excited squeals.

As he approached the stage, I gasped. I jumped from the platform and bellied up to him. Forgetting about my lapel microphone, I sputtered, "Santa, XYZ!"

He lifted a shoulder and cocked a brow, then shrugged and sang obligingly, "A-B-C-D . . ."

Horrified, and wide-eyed, I hissed, "Santa, XYZ!"

"E-F-G, H-I-J-K, L-M-N-O . . ."

"Stop singing!" I could see the confusion in his eyes. "XYZ! Examine. Your. Zipper. Fix your pants," I shrilled.

In his haste to get dressed, Bill had cinched the fur of his jacket into his belt. I tugged it down over his gaping pants. Thank heavens he'd worn jeans underneath.

"Don't you know what XYZ stands for?" I muttered in his ear.

"Nope," he whispered back. "In my day, we said, 'The barn door's open.'"

Well, the children had promised to "leave the door open." But I never thought Santa would, too!

Christmas in July

By *Todd Outcalt*

I n July of 1997, I received a phone call from a social worker.

"I'm a visiting nurse," she said, "and every Tuesday morning I help a young lady named Myra who is homebound. She listens to your radio broadcast on Sunday mornings and was wondering if you might find time to stop by and see her this week?"

As a pastor, I often get these requests, but this one seemed different. "Certainly," I said. "Give me the address, and I'll stop by this afternoon."

On the drive to that part of town that hot day, I made my way past ramshackle houses and a plethora of junkyard dogs and abandoned cars. I slipped along rows of shotgun houses until I found the address and eased my car into a small opening in the barren yard.

I rang the bell on the front porch and was instantly greeted by a shout from the belly of the tiny house. I inched open the door and walked inside where Myra—probably in her early thirties—reclined on a gigantic bed. It was fitted with a system of ropes, pulleys, and lifts, all designed to hoist her limp body from the bed to a waiting wheelchair.

"Are you the pastor I listen to on Sunday mornings?"

"Yes, I suppose I am." I drifted to her side to introduce myself. "It's a pleasure to meet you, Myra."

Slowly, she lifted a palsied hand and smiled. "Thank you . . . for visiting." Each word was a struggle that brought her to the edge of breathlessness. "I wanted . . . to give you . . . a gift."

Although pastors often receive gifts, I was startled. It was clear that Myra could not walk, could barely lift a hand, and that some dreadful disease had been siphoning her strength for years, taking her day by day, week by week, until her body had been reduced to helplessness. I felt at once guilty and awkward, wondering what she could possibly have to spare—and how I could accept a present from this dear woman.

"I love the radio broadcast," she said. "I am your most . . . faithful listener."

"You might be the *only* listener," I joked.

She smiled. "Look behind you."

The living room was sparse—a cube containing a small couch, a television set on a stand, a wooden stool. I saw stacks of neglected magazines and dusty books, a hodgepodge of family photographs tacked to the wall . . . and a Christmas tree filled with angels.

"I keep my tree up year round," she answered at the questioning lift of my brows. "It's always Christmas . . . in this house."

"That's wonderful," I said, my hesitation obvious.

"I have more than five hundred angels in my collection."

Indeed, branches on the artificial tree bent under the weight. Angels made of ceramic, tin, and wood. Angels fashioned from paper, wings thin as gossamer, ready to soar toward the heavens. There were angels with halos. Angels with glowing faces. Angels with feet of clay. Some did not look like angels at all— but had sad, circumspect, and fully human faces. Others had arms outstretched and welcoming. Angels of laughter. Of joy. Of mercy.

"I've never seen so many in one place," I admitted. "They are beautiful."

"I want . . . to give you one," Myra said.

How could I pluck an angel from her beloved tree? "Oh, I couldn't disturb your collection."

"Please take one."

"I couldn't."

"It's . . . a gift."

A gift. Yes. But . . . "It isn't Christmas," I said.

"It is always . . . Christmas."

I padded toward the tree, paused to consider the choices. The angels smiled, shimmered, seemed to lift me with hovering wings. I would take a small one—the tiniest, the most homely, the least of these. Reaching toward the back of the tree I plucked a small rosebud angel from its perch—a cherub with hands folded, eyes closed, deep in prayer.

I showed it to Myra, asking permission with my gaze.

"That's little Tommy," she said. "He is saying a prayer for you."

"Thank you," I murmured.

"Take him . . . home with you."

I edged back to Myra's bedside, still uncomfortable with the idea of accepting the gift. The only thing I could offer in return was a prayer. And so we prayed, amid a Christmas in July, the giver and the gift.

"May I visit you again?" I asked when it was time for me to leave.

"Yes, please," she said. "Come see me . . . again soon."

I saw Myra many times during the next dozen years. At each visit, however, she insisted I select a cherub from her Christmas tree to take home and add to my collection—my growing collection—of angels.

And they are still with me, those symbols of heaven.

As is Myra, with earthly angels in the form of friends and family and nurses—guardians who watch over her, steadying her hands, tending her fragile body, recognizing that *she* is the real gift. Myra, who bears witness to the unseen grace that moves the world and lifts us beyond the shadows of this life.

Myra, a woman who teaches me that it is always Christmas. Even in July.

Up Front

By Terri Elders

Even though Mama always warned me to be careful what I wished for, I had no doubt I wanted a padded bra for Christmas. I wished for one when I blew out the candles on my twelfth birthday and again when I split the Thanksgiving wishbone with my sister. Once I even sneaked outside late at night to search for a falling star to wish on, too.

I had skipped a grade at school, so felt dwarfed by the other girls in seventh grade who wore bras, whether they needed them or not. I'd seen a few girls in the restroom stuffing Kleenex for extra filler, but in the gym showers I recognized that most already had no need for such artifice. I did.

I'd heard of training bras but thought that sounded like something for wannabe ten-year-olds, just one step up from an undershirt. I longed for the real article, a lacy 32AA with some slight padding to give me the illusion of curves. My older sister Patti had bras, and I wanted one, too.

Actually, *wanted* might be too mild a word to describe how incredibly desperate I was to be able to look down and see something other than my slightly knobby knees. I pined, I yearned, and I hankered and hungered. Sometimes, at night, I'd pat a hand across my concave chest as I called for divine intervention.

"Not too big," I'd whisper, "just a little something to distinguish me from my brother."

At first, my parents scoffed at my request. "Christmas is a time for games, for things you really need. Like coats, for example, not underwear," Mama said.

"Bra? That's silly," Daddy said.

Patti agreed that she, for one, needed a new coat, a pea jacket just like the other girls were sporting that winter.

But I whined and wheedled, moaned and groaned, until finally Mama sighed and shook her head. "We'll think about it."

Daddy grumbled, but I knew I had won. When Mama thought about something, it got well thought about, and I knew she wanted me to be happy. And to look nice. Just like she always reminded me to wear clean shorts when I went to play tennis and to wash my hair when I came home from the playground pool.

On Christmas morning, Patti opened her present first, the biggest box under the tree. She pulled out a navy blue pea jacket and squealed with delight. She threw it on and vamped around the living room as if she were parading down a catwalk. I had to admit she looked chic indeed in the broad-lapelled coat with its slash pockets and big wooden buttons.

My old red wool would get me through another winter, I told myself, even though I had noticed it was getting snug across the shoulders. I reached for my package, much smaller, but gaily wrapped. I opened the box and spied, nestled among the tissue, not one, but two delicate brassieres.

My father and brother looked the other way when I pulled them from the box, but Mama and Patti smiled. I scampered into the bedroom to try one on and nearly cried for joy when I saw myself in the mirror. I had a bosom at long, long last. For the next few hours I preened, pretending not to notice my brother's knowing smirks.

Later that day we prepared for the drive to Grandma's for Christmas dinner. Since the temperature in late December had dipped into the low forties, cold for Southern California, I threw on my old red jacket. But when I started to button it up I realized I had a problem. No matter how hard I tugged, the buttons wouldn't slip into the buttonholes. They were about half an inch shy.

The culprit was my Christmas bra. The padding added just enough girth to my front to render the coat unclosable. And red wool did not fall into the category of a stretch fabric.

I had a choice—either remove the bra or go to Grandma's coatless. I chose the latter, yanking the army blanket from my bed and wrapping it around my shoulders. Nobody said anything when we piled into the backseat, but I couldn't help noticing how pretty and warm Patti looked in her new coat.

Grandma marveled at my enhanced figure. "She's really growing up," she said, even though she'd seen me the week before and must have known I couldn't develop that fast. Grandpa did a silent double take.

When school started after winter break, I decided to put the bras aside until the weather got warmer. I couldn't substitute my army blanket on the long hike to the bus, so would have to button my jacket against the chill. I thought about tucking a bra into my zipper notebook and sneaking into the restroom before classes, but remembered how embarrassed those girls had looked when I saw them with the Kleenex. I decided not to make myself a laughing-stock. The bras would wait for their school debut.

By spring I had grown two inches and gained ten pounds. On the first day balmy enough to head for the bus without my old jacket, I eagerly pulled one of the bras from the drawer where they had languished all winter. *So pretty,* I thought as I stuck my arms through the straps and reached behind to fasten the hooks.

It wouldn't hook. I took it off and stared at it in disbelief. The 32AA was now too small. Then my eye fell on something else, something softly rounded.

"Be careful what you wish for," Mama had said.

Thank heavens my birthday was coming up soon. I knew exactly what to wish for. A new jacket in a larger size. Because it was suddenly clear that Mama and I would have to go to the store for underwear before then. Probably right away!

Owed to Joy

By Ted Thompson

Shelly was the perfect age for Christmas: old enough to under-stand the true meaning of the season, but still completely enchanted by the magic of it. Her innocent joyfulness was com-pelling and catching, and a great gift to parents, reminding us what Christmas should represent no matter how old we are.

The most highly prized gift Shelly received on Christmas Eve was a giant bubble-maker. It was a simple device of plastic and cloth that the inventor promised would create huge, billowing bubbles large enough to swallow our wide-eyed four-year-old. Both Shelly and I were excited about trying it out, but it was after dark so we'd have to wait until the next day.

That night after all the gifts had been opened, I read the instruction booklet while Shelly played with some of her other new toys. The inventor of the bubble-maker had tried all types of soaps for formulating bubbles and had found that Joy dish-washing detergent created the best giant bubbles. I'd have to buy some.

The next morning I was awakened early by small stirrings in the house. Shelly was up. I knew in my sleepy mind that Christmas

Day could be held back no longer, so I rose and made my way toward the kitchen to start the coffee.

In the hallway I met my tiny daughter, already wide awake, the bubble-maker clutched in her chubby little hand, the wonder of Christmas morning embraced in her young heart.

"Daddy, can we make bubbles now?" Her eyes sparkled with excitement.

I sighed heavily. I rubbed my eyes. I looked toward the window where the sky was only beginning to lighten with the dawn. I looked toward the kitchen where the coffeepot had yet to start dripping.

"Shelly," I said, my voice almost pleading, and perhaps a little annoyed, "It's too early. I haven't even had my coffee yet."

Her smile fell away. Immediately, I felt a father's remorse for bursting her bright Christmas bubble with what she must have seen as my own selfish problem, and my heart broke a little.

But I was a grown-up. I could fix this. In a flash of adult inspiration, I unloaded the responsibility. Recalling the inventor's recommendation of a particular brand of bubble-making detergent—which I knew we did not have in the house—I laid the blame squarely on him, pointing out gently, "Besides, Shelly, you have to have Joy."

I watched her eyes light up again as she realized in less than an instant that she could neutralize this small problem with the great and wonderful truth she had to reveal.

"Oh, Daddy," she pledged, glowing with honesty and enthusiasm and Christmas excitement, "Oh, Daddy, I do."

I broke records getting to the store, and in no time at all we were out on the front lawn creating gigantic, billowing, gossamer orbs—each one conjured of purest Joy, and sent forth shimmering in the Christmas sun.

Of Evergreens and Fake Firs: The Trees We've Known and Loved

All in a Row

By Anne Culbreath Watkins

My father is the gruff, outdoorsy type who prefers hiking through the woods to sitting sedately inside a stuffy house. At eighty years old, Daddy has a mind of his own and is quick to set straight anyone who dares suggest he slow down. He is stubborn and not a man prone to displays of sentimentality. Yet despite this brusque demeanor, he never passes up a chance to celebrate the holidays with family.

After one celebratory meal at my brother's house, we all decided to walk off the calories. We strolled around the property while Daddy reminisced about the old place where we'd all grown up. Situated mere feet from my brother's home, the rickety frame house was long gone, but there were still plenty of things to look at in the yard that once surrounded it.

Daddy pointed toward a scraggly row of cedars, each one bigger than the other. "Do you remember what those are?" he asked.

An unexpected crush of memories transported me to Christmases past, when artificial trees played no part in our holidays. Every year we decorated a living tree—hauled, complete with root-ball, from the woods by my father.

The tree always stood in the corner of the front room, sticky-prickly branches dripping with glowing lights, sentimental ornaments, and tinsel. Daddy propped the tree in a bucket of water to keep it alive. Before he plugged in the lights each day, I enjoyed sitting beneath it, swirling my fingers in the cool depths and inhaling the piney aroma.

As soon as Christmas was over, Daddy took the tree outside and planted it in the front yard where it joined a row of other cedars, memorials to holidays gone by, that grew into a thick wall I loved to play behind. It shielded me from cars passing on the street close by and provided a fragrant shelter.

When I was six, we moved to Alabama, leaving behind the woodsy screen. I wondered if Christmas there would be as wonderful as those in Ohio. Would Santa know where to bring our presents? Would the little Nativity scene look out of place? Could we even have Christmas without snow? But Daddy stepped in.

One December day, he disappeared into the woods and returned a short time later carrying a small, shapely cedar he set in a bucket in the living room. We decorated it with the same ornaments saved from holidays past, along with colorful paper chains and stars we cut from construction paper. Wise men smiled from the Nativity scene, pleased to celebrate the Christ child's birthday with us in Alabama. And I told myself Santa would find us no matter where we were.

On Christmas morning, gaily wrapped gifts appeared under the tree, and stockings filled with goodies hung heavy near the crackling woodstove. The day was as wonderful as I'd hoped, even without any snow. And after the holidays, just like he had in Ohio, Daddy took our Christmas tree outside.

Easing the root-ball from the bucket, he planted it beside the house where it eventually grew into a beautiful, full-bodied tree. Each year he added another until there was a tapered line of cedars—like those we left behind in Ohio—standing point over our Alabama house.

My father had grown up in a home where Christmas gifts were few and far between, and whatever holiday sentimentality he may have harbored was stuffed deeply beneath the surface. Yet, somehow he hit upon the one thing that proved how much the season meant to him. Long after Daddy is gone, those trees will stand there, a living testimony to the warm heart nestled inside the quiet, sometimes curt old man.

And they'll remind me that there is much more to Christmas than decorations, presents, Santa Claus, and snow.

Tinsel Time

By Joanne Hirase-Stacey

What a glorious holiday it would be. After four years, my husband Bill and I finally decided to get a real Christmas tree. We'd never had one before because our house was small and we didn't want the hassle of storing decorations.

In the past, we'd had tabletop trees—a fake ten-incher with a burlap sack wrapping the bottom, a gold wire spiraling to a peak, and a green wooden triangle flecked with bright colors. We lit pine-scented candles and sprayed our wreath with eucalyptus oil, but it wasn't the same as having the woodsy scent of a live tree.

The bushy evergreen we selected fit perfectly into a corner. I gently opened new boxes of ornaments, and we hung each fragile decoration with great care. Globe by colorful globe, our tree took on its unique look.

"Where's the garland?" Bill looked around.

"I didn't buy any."

"We need some gold garland."

I dug through the bag lying at my feet and pulled out two small boxes. I handed one to him.

"Tinsel?" He made a face.

"I love tinsel. It's fun to throw it on the tree and let it land wherever, then straighten it so it hangs just right."

"It's droopy, stringy, and old-fashioned. No one uses tinsel."

I opened my box, grabbed a small handful, and tossed it at the tree. Then I carefully moved the silver strands so they draped nicely over a branch.

"See? It's beautiful."

He handed me his box and left to watch television.

After I finished decorating, I dragged Bill back into our living room.

"It doesn't look too bad." He tugged on some tinsel.

"Thanks. If we have a real tree again next year, I'll get garland," I promised. "Any color you want."

Since I'd already wrapped my husband's presents, I hauled them from the closet and arranged them on the glittery tree skirt. The space looked bare, so I decided to wrap the other gifts we'd bought and put them under the tree as well. Presents for family, friends, and the girls (our dogs) completed the festive scene.

Hands on hips, I stood back to admire my handiwork. "It looks like a picture straight out of a magazine."

Bill brought the dogs into the room to see the tree. Cindy and Honey sniffed a few branches and walked away. Lucille and Abigail took their sweet time, nudging ornaments with their noses and snuffling presents. When they decided the tree was disinteresting and nonthreatening, they moseyed back to their beds.

A few days later, Bill called me at work. "When are you coming home?"

"My usual time, why?"

"You'd better be prepared to see what your girls did." Amazing how the foursome always became my dogs when they were naughty.

I hurried home—and found my beautiful tree in the middle of the floor, new ornaments shattered and pine needles scattered, several presents torn open. I couldn't believe my eyes.

None of our friends or family will get to enjoy our masterpiece, I mourned. Tearfully, I put the dogs outside and cleaned up the mess. I knew the neighbors would wonder why our tree was stuffed in the garbage can, lights and all.

"Mom is mad at you, Lucy," Bill chastised our little pit bull. "You wrecked the tree."

"Cindy and Honey wouldn't have done it," I agreed. They were older and never got into any trouble. "It could have been Abby, though. Why are you blaming Lucy?"

"The evidence points at her."

Curious, I cupped Lucy's sweet face in my hands, but I didn't see any telltale sign pointing at her as the number one suspect.

"Uh, you're looking at the wrong end." Bill tried not to laugh.

I turned Lucy around and saw it—tinsel peeping out beneath her tail.

"The vet said not to pull." Bill handed me an old pair of scissors. "You just have to keep it trimmed until there isn't any more."

I took the scissors and eyed Lucy with reluctance.

"I hate to say it," Bill paused for effect, "but you should have gotten garland!"

Visions of Tree Trimming Dance in Our Heads

By Marybeth Hicks

We're trying to get into the spirit of the season, but we repeat the mistake of planning idyllic experiences—which, of course, ruin the coming of Christmas. Case in point: trimming the tree. For years I tried to eliminate all potential reasons why tree trimming could become (how to put this?) an evening in the fires of hell.

Once, when our children were little, we created an idyllic afternoon in which we planned to explore the local Christmas tree farm, choose a majestic fir, spruce, or pine (who can tell, really?), and drive home with the perfect Christmas tree tied to the roof of our family van. All the while, we would sing carols in unison. (Or would harmony be more ideal?)

Don't be shocked, but it didn't turn out that way.

If I recall correctly, the temperature was something like fifteen degrees. I wrapped the children in so many layers that they couldn't move their arms and legs. Inexplicably, I dressed them in single pairs of flimsy cotton socks and inadequate snow boots (made of a substance not found in nature and unequal to the task of warming their feet).

"I'm cold," a child griped seven seconds after we got out of the van and walked (or waddled, as the case may be) toward the wagon that would drop us in the forest.

"At least you have the good mittens. My hands are frozen," another chimed in.

The complaining escalated.

"You always get the good mittens."

"That's because you lost the other mittens."

And then, one of the children said the wrong thing. "Why is this taking so long?"

Of course, it was taking so long because my husband was in search of the one and only evergreen with a straight tree trunk. For reasons beyond my comprehension, he operated under the misconception that there really is such a thing.

From that moment on, our ideal afternoon on the tree farm dwindled into an exercise in frozen futility. I worried that the baby was at risk for hypothermia, so I did what all wives do when we know we're running out of time and the demands of motherhood are about to collide head-on with the responsibilities of being a good spouse: I flattered my husband's taste in trees.

"Honey, you're right, that clearly is the tree that Joseph himself would have chosen had he not been so busy finding a stable for Mary. It's a winner."

He tested my sincerity. "Are you sure?"

"Can we go now?" warbled a chilled cherub.

"Absolutely," I assured. "It's the perfect tree."

Yeah, right. You know what happened next because it has happened to you or someone you know. Even if you don't celebrate

Christmas, you've probably experienced the equivalent in furniture assembly or wallpapering.

We got home and Jim cut the bottom so it would drink water from the tree stand (assuming we remembered to refill the stand with water). This was standard operating procedure, after all. But cutting the bottom caused the tree to list to one side, so naturally he cut a little more. And a little more. And more still.

Eventually, we stood in the family room next to a three-foot Christmas bush.

If memory serves me correctly, Jim and I had an argument. I fed the children a can of soup and some watery hot cocoa. He put the little ones to bed with a promise to trim the tree the next day; I left to purchase a professionally cut pine from the vendor on the vacant lot near the gas station.

Tears. Apologies. Forgiveness. Merry Christmas.

On December 26 a few years later, I bought a six-foot artificial blue spruce on clearance, put it in the storage room, and smugly planned the perfect family tree trimming experience for the following year. At least I would eliminate a needle-clogged vacuum cleaner and potential sap stains.

The six of us still believe that tree trimming is an idyllic experience despite annual tensions and conflict. And this year was no exception.

When we pulled out our trusty artificial tree, someone (no one pointed fingers) had tangled the lights so inextricably into the boughs of plastic and wire that the plug disappeared. While my husband and I tussled with the lights, the kids unwrapped—and broke—several glass Santas.

Tears. Apologies. Forgiveness. Merry Christmas.

For whatever reason, our collective imaginations still harbor a fantasy of family togetherness that's only possible in a Frank Capra movie. Then again, every year is somehow more idyllic than the last, even if we're writing the script ourselves.

The Finest Christmas Tree

Christopher Garry

Christmas tree, ah, Christmas tree
standing in the hall,
so dressed up with ornaments
. . . you're just about to fall.

Angels, snowflakes, balls, and stars,
all turning round and round.
I see my favorite keepsake
has fallen to the ground.

Lights of gold and green and white
and flashing ones of red,
the crooked star of Bethlehem
high above my head.

The needles seem to pile up
all around the floor.
I want to add another ball,
but I can't fit no more.

Christmas tree, ah, Christmas tree
leaning on the wall,
though you are not perfect,
you are the finest tree of all.

THE PERFECT
TREE

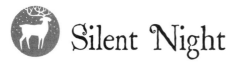# Silent Night

By Carla Zwahlen

Buying a Christmas tree, I reminded myself, *was not going to get any easier no matter how long I procrastinated.* I lost track of how many times I'd passed the tree lot without stopping. I could not miss the display. It stood next to the post office where I picked up my mail every day.

Six months ago, cancer stole my beautiful husband from me. As the cutting edge of loss clipped the threads that bound me to Werner, I isolated one of loss's blatant characteristics: Firsts. Doing things for the first time without Werner.

As the minutes ticked away, these Firsts automatically laced themselves throughout my everyday steps. Even though some were easier than others to get through, I felt the jagged-edged hole that Werner's death left in my life. Even the smallest things he did for me, the ones I took for granted, became a confrontation with loss.

Buying the Christmas tree was especially difficult; I feared the emotional encounter awaiting me at the tree lot. I worried and argued with myself, until a quiet voice in my head reminded me, *Christmas Eve is nearly here.* The thought of telling my family there would be no tree this year bothered me.

By itself, the evergreen was not special. But enveloping it was a thirty-three-year-old Swiss tradition that Werner and his sons, Stefan and Jurg, carried out—a ritual they anticipated. In all those years, I had never selected or bought the tree.

I drove to the lot.

I took a deep breath, stepped out of my car, and walked between the rows of balsam and spruce. The heavy, woodsy aroma caught me and lifted me to another time and another row of trees years earlier, when Stefan was only three.

Stefan had insisted on carrying the big shovel and struggled to hold the fat handle in his hands. He dragged it through tall field grass and into the forest. Every few steps, the shovel slipped from his tiny grasp and slid to the ground. He stopped, picked it up, and marched on toward his important mission—choosing a little balsam for his dad.

Stefan examined each tree, while I told him about the Christmases of Werner's childhood in Switzerland. "Santa Claus does not visit the Swiss children's homes." Stefan frowned at the thought. "However, a week before Christmas, on Saint Nicholas day, the Swiss children receive chocolate and special cookies to eat. They save Christmas Eve just for the celebration of Jesus's birth." Stefan's face brightened.

I told him how his dad's family visited the forest to find their tree. When Christmas Eve arrived, they placed the little balsam in their living room and decorated it with oranges and homemade ornaments. They clipped candle holders onto the branch tips and placed short tapers into each one.

"After dinner they sang carols," I told Stephan, "and each

person helped light the candles. Once all the candles burned bright, they sang 'Stille Nacht.' It reminded them that Jesus is the true light and savior in a dark world."

Stefan chose a three-foot balsam while he listened to my story. With help from me, he dug into the dirt and wrested the tree from the ground. We nestled the root-ball into the black nursery pot I carried. At home, we hid the tree behind the woodshed and hoped it remained a secret until Christmas Eve.

The day before Christmas, we waited until Werner went to work and, like two jolly conspirators, we decorated the tree. We looped red and white paper chains around the needles, hung the little white candles on the branch tips, and hid the tree again. Stefan worked hard to contain his excitement while he waited to present his dad with a "Swiss Christmas tree."

That evening, Stefan and I slipped from the house and gathered the tree we had decorated in the colors of Switzerland. We placed it on the big granite step outside the front door, lit the candles—and hoped the wind did not snuff them out.

Candlelight danced against the darkness and illuminated the big smile on Stefan's face. We pounded on the door and shouted, "Merry Christmas!"

Werner opened the door and gaped at the two of us standing there. When his eyes rested on the candlelit tree, a smile spread across his face and reached far into that holy Christmas night.

Every year after our first "Swiss Christmas Eve," Werner, Stefan, and Jurg carried a tree from the forest and set it in our big solar greenhouse. On Christmas Eve, family and friends gathered for a special dinner and carols while we lit candles on the tree.

Candlelight danced up and down the long windows and spread across each smiling face. For a moment, when all the candles burned, the room hushed. And then the caroling began.

When the last strains of "O Tannenbaum" faded, Werner's clear baritone lifted up the notes of "Stille Nacht," his gift to us.

But now Werner was gone and I had to accomplish my task alone.

After some consideration, I chose a fat balsam. *How will I ever lift this tree onto my car roof?* I worried.

I hardly finished the thought when the owner of the tree lot approached. "You are not going to put this tree on your car. I will call my husband to have him deliver it to your house."

It was a small town. People knew.

"Thank you," I said aloud, even as I sent a silent thanks to God for sheltering me from the experience of carrying the tree home alone.

Christmas Eve arrived with the tree in its place. Family and friends gathered for a special dinner. Later we sang as we lit the candles. We rejoiced and remembered the first still and holy night, when God sent his only Son to be our light in this dark world. The birth of Jesus centered us on our first Christmas celebration without Werner.

Candlelight flickered against glass and spread its glow across the faces of family and friends. The room hushed, but no one sang "Stille Nacht." Instead, we stood for a moment of silence, each person not ready yet for that First.

Perhaps next year . . .

The Too-Tall Tree

By Peggy Frezon

Daylight was fading as we pulled into the Christmas tree lot. *Maybe it's closed,* I thought hopefully. But festive white bulbs strung across the entrance were still lit.

Usually, I couldn't wait to get our tree and decorate it with Mike and the kids. I loved the big old-fashioned lights, the hand-me-down glass ornaments, and the sparkling silver tinsel we hung one strand at a time. At night, we turned off all the lights in the house and sat around the tree, mesmerized by its twinkling colors. Even Kate, eighteen, and Andy, fourteen, weren't too old to enjoy the spirit of this simple holiday tradition.

But this year, the cherished ritual didn't seem so simple. It wasn't that I didn't want a tree. It was just, well—the size. My husband insisted a proper Christmas tree must at least skim the ceiling. Our snug, older house was far from large, but the ceilings were more than ten feet high. And a ten-foot pine tended to get pretty bushy, with branches that could easily take over an entire living room.

"Maybe we could try a smaller tree this year," I suggested as everyone tumbled out of the van. I envisioned a simple little evergreen on a table in the corner.

A man with tan coveralls and thick boots approached.

"Could you point us toward the Fraser firs?" Mike asked and added, "The big ones?" My heart sank.

We followed the man to a row of fragrant firs leaning against a rough wooden frame. "Here's a real big one." He grasped a tree with his heavy gloves. Mike stretched his arm high to gauge the height and smiled.

"It looks a little, uh, tall." I tried desperately to point everyone toward the more reasonably sized pines in front. But before I knew it, they were admiring a tree with *that look* on their faces.

I gazed up and up—and up. "Wait! It's too tall!"

The kids' rosy faces beamed. Mike glowed with satisfaction. The coveralled man waited expectantly.

Feeling like Scrooge, I sighed and thought of the stack of greeting cards to sign, the cookies to bake, the errands to run. Wouldn't trimming twice the tree take twice the time? Still, my family wanted this tree. I didn't have the heart to cause a fuss.

At home, Mike dragged the fir through the back door, and I gasped as branches compressed and squeezed through the slender frame. *Oh no! Where could we put this giant redwood?*

In the past, we had tried various locations for oversized trees, but bushy greenery was always in the way.

"I could rearrange the furniture," Mike offered. He moved a chair onto the porch and dragged the couch, loveseat, and coffee table against the far wall. I scowled at the inconvenience Mike's tree was causing. This was not the simple Christmas I wanted.

Mike tugged the enormous fir into the newly freed corner. It looked like we were on the *Titanic* and all the furniture had slid to one end.

The mood was as icy as the frigid winter weather outside. I felt anything but jolly and bright. I pouted like a child who had found coal in her stocking. Angry words were on the tip of my tongue: *I told you so. I told you not to get a big tree. I told you it wouldn't fit!* But I stopped myself.

The kids had long since scattered. And Mike—Mike looked like a man who was trying to provide his family with a memorable Christmas in the best way he knew. I read the disappointment in his eyes.

I knew without a doubt that what happened next was totally in my control. I could react in anger and spew out those hateful words—*I told you so*—or I could ignore the minor inconveniences and rejoice in the grandeur of the grand fir. I took a deep breath and surveyed the space again.

It's not important enough to ruin Christmas, I decided. I felt the tenseness in my muscles relax. "How about if we try it over there?" I pointed.

"It will be in the way," Mike warned softly.

I nodded. "That's okay."

"We'll have to shove the dining table up against the wall."

I was silent for a moment. "I can live with that."

When all the pushing and pulling was done, our eleven-foot tree stood in the back of the dining room, branches jutting out crazily every which way. Although it took up half the room, the tree was elegant and beautifully proportioned. Its piney scent smelled like Christmas.

It took us all night and fifteen strings of big old-fashioned bulbs to fill the tree. Hundreds of special ornaments adorned the boughs. Mike placed the old cloth angel at the top. She gazed down, reminding me of a central focus I had forgotten. How silly of me to have overlooked the more important meaning of Christmas.

That night, the whole family snuggled in the dark, admiring colorful lights, hand-blown glass ornaments, and glittery tinsel. It didn't matter that the furniture was cramped to one side or that we constantly banged our heads on the dangling chandelier that used to be isolated by the placement of the dining table.

We had our tree and—big or small, tucked out of the way or inconveniently placed—it just didn't matter. Our family tradition lived on. Christmas hadn't been simple, but it was simply perfect.

 For tips on finding the perfect tree, see page 183.

Out on a Limb

By Andrea Langworthy

My husband and I bought a fake Christmas tree. Pre-lit, with tiny clear lights. We'd talked about it for years. Every time he dragged the remains of a Fraser fir through the house and out the sliding glass door opening. After he'd hoisted it over the deck and pulled it up the hill in time for the sanitation company to haul it away. It was a hot topic when I vacuumed millions of fallen needles from the carpet. By the time each new holiday season rolled around, though, we forgot the hassles.

Until this year.

We searched for the perfect tree with the perfect price tag. Sticker shock isn't just for automobiles, we learned. Our budget rose as we shopped.

"That one," we finally said.

I worried needlessly about fitting the nine-foot tree in our car. The waist-high carton slid easily into our midsized Malibu.

"How many limbs are there?" I wondered.

"We'll see," my husband said.

By the time we put sections A through E together, the tree was much bigger than it had looked in the store. "We have to return it for a smaller one," I said. "But how will we ever get it back into the box?"

My husband said not to decide until each of the branches was pulled apart. Raising my voice to frenzy level, I explained what any sane person could plainly see—it was too big for the room.

"Let's see," he said. An hour later, when every branch fanned out and each needle was in place, he advised me to sleep on the decision. I did, awaking hourly in a panic.

In the morning, I poked my head into the living room and repeated that the tree was too oversized for our house. Hubby announced his intention to get on the ladder and start looping ribbons around the tree. I told him there wouldn't be enough. He repeated his "let's see" mantra and unrolled the spools of red and gold trim, suggesting I find the angel for the top. I wailed that the angel was too small to be nine-feet skyward.

"Let's see," he said. Then he left for work, leaving me alone with a tree that had taken over the whole room and was about to crowd me out of the house.

That night, I said we should remove the garlands and get the tree back to the store. My husband decided to put ornaments on some of the top boughs—to keep the angel company.

"We'll need binoculars to see them up there," I said. He thought we should wait and see.

Even though it would be added work to remove them before we returned the tree, when he hurried to work the next day, I hung a few things on lower limbs. Just to prove how silly they would look. Surely my husband would come to his senses, disassemble the mighty oak, and return it to the store.

I hung angels a neighbor had given me and a snowman from a friend alongside framed photos of our grandchildren. When it was dark outside, I plugged in the lights and stepped back to look at the gargantuan evergreen.

The bright bulbs made mirrored ornaments from my father twinkle and bells from my mother glimmer. They glowed through brightly colored glass decorations created by my children. As memories of Christmases past enveloped the room, I phoned my husband.

"It's safe to come home," I said. "The tree's staying. In fact, I might just leave it up all year long."

Christmas Outside the Box: Offbeat and Untraditional Celebrations

Oy, Come All Ye Faithful

By Dorri Olds

"How would you feel about Dad and I sleeping over Christmas Eve and we all go out for breakfast Christmas Day?" A trap, a snare. In Mom's world, my feelings have nothing to do with anything. Especially when she wants something, which is all the time.

See, I'm a dedicated homebody. I live in a one-bedroom apartment that, okay, I admit—I wouldn't even have if they hadn't spent a *fortune* putting me through college. But them sleeping over? Give up my firm queen mattress, down pillows, and Calvin Klein silky-soft leopard-print sheets?

If I say no it'll trigger, "*This*—to your own mother? After all we've . . ." The guilt will eat at me until next Christmas.

Two options: sleep in the other room on the floor on an air mattress (rather have weasels rip my flesh), or sleep on the couch, which is right next to the bed (nightmares of being tied to her by an umbilical cord). It's hard enough to create boundaries without us sleeping like sardines.

"Okay, Mom. Sure."

We're devout atheist Jews. Dad taught me passionately, "Religion was created by the rich to control the masses. Poor dumb people, manipulated by their own fears." Our family celebrates every holiday—Christmas, Hanukkah, Easter, Passover. "Oy, how we've suffered, now let's eat."

Mom and Dad arrive early and buzz from the lobby three times. I've told them once is plenty. Buddy barks and runs in frenzied circles. They ring my doorbell twice, and knock, then call out, "Hi, we're here."

Okay, breathe. Grant me the serenity to accept the parents I cannot change.

"Hi Mom! Hi Dad!"

"Hi honey!"

I smile the way I do when Dad's setting the camera for our annual family pictures and my nieces are crying while Dad is shouting damnitsmile.

Jogging three miles a day for forty years shows in Mom's taut, muscular legs. The stubborn bulge in her tummy looks out of place on her otherwise lithe body. Mom's short, curly hair looks whiter than I remember, contrasted by thick black eyebrows— her lethal weapons.

I love Dad's olive skin, even at eighty-eight, with its thin folds and neat creases. I marvel at his lean, muscular body. He's never fluctuated more than three pounds. He still plays tennis twice a week. I can tell by the way he's standing that his shoulder hurts.

"Lookin' good there, kid. Boy, I wanna tell you, if I was twenty years younger and not your father, you'd be in trouble." He pats me on the rear even though I've told him three thousand times not to.

They drop their coats over chairs and Mom plops her huge purse onto the table with a forceful clunk and squishes the perfectly folded napkins.

My jaw is so tight I'll have to call the chiropractor later.

"Honey," Mom says in her shrill nasal voice, "I brought you some clippings."

One of the things I love about Mom is that she mails articles to me with bright yellow Post-it notes, "Enjoy!" or "FYI" and always "Love, Mom." It's so sweet it makes me want to cry, but right now I'm timing the vegetables and the pasta and the chicken, and I can't give her my attention.

"Let's talk about it after dinner, Ma."

She lets out a sigh and shoots me a look. I return to the kitchen and call out, "Can you please clear your stuff off the table and chairs? Dinner's almost ready."

Mom follows me and says, "How can I help?"

I know she means well, but she's oblivious. When she walks into the narrow kitchen it cramps me into a corner—the antithesis to help. I have shooting pains in my neck and a burning sensation in my arms. My right eye twitches. Dad walks into the kitchen. Now I really can't move.

Dinner is pleasant enough. My shoulders lower a little. *Okay. I'm going to be alright.*

We go to the couch. Mom starts talking about her recent three-day silent retreat. The entire time she attended it was quiet. Nobody spoke as they ate together, meditated, walked trails. Mom yaks for an hour about the virtue of silence.

At last they tire. I dream of being chased by monsters—naked and frozen in place by cemented feet.

Okay, it's morning. Mom's in the bathroom. Rats. I make myself a double shot of espresso—I'm going to need it.

Mom comes out perky. "Merry Christmas!"

I have a crick in my neck. I take two Advil and hope for the best.

Dad is waking up slowly. Noise doesn't disturb him. Without hearing aids in, he's stone deaf. His hairpiece needs a comb. I notice his barrel chest is all gray as he shuffles to the bathroom in his white jockey shorts.

"Merry Christmas." I smile—genuinely this time.

Then she starts, "What long-distance carrier do you use?"

"Um, I don't know, Ma, why?"

"Because you're paying too much."

"Oh."

"He-llo-o?" Her tone rattles windows.

"Yes, Mom, I'm right here." I sound like a weary kindergarten teacher.

"Well? What long-distance carrier do you use?"

"I said, I don't know."

"What do you mean you don't know?!" Her veiny hand, propped on her slender hip, feels like it's around my neck, choking the life out of me.

"Mom, not now."

"You don't know which carrier you use?"

"It's early, I haven't had breakfast, and I don't care about this now."

I'm sure there was irritation in my voice, but not enough to warrant her throwing on her clothes, storming out, and letting the door slam behind her.

"Well now you've done it!" Dad says. He glares at me

"What?" I whimper. "I didn't do anything."

"You upset your mother."

"Da-ad. Please, don't get mad."

"Well, it's too late for that, isn't it?"

I reluctantly pull on clothes, feeling grubby without my morning shower. We go downstairs. The doorman points to Mom sulking. As soon as she sees us she bolts up the block, stomping her feet in her big red boots. It's hard not to laugh. By suppressing my laughter, years of heartbreaking family dramas well up in my throat.

"Where's she going?" I say to Dad, making sure it's loud enough for her to hear.

"Shhhh," he snaps at me. "Come on. We have to catch up to her."

"You go ahead, Dad. I'll meet you at the corner."

He shakes his head dramatically, muttering, "Incomprehensible," and goes after her. I see Dad talking to her and Mom flailing her arms. They wait for me at the light.

"So," I say, trying to sound chipper, "Where would you like to go for Christmas breakfast?"

Nobody answers. I suggest a nice place nearby. I hear a couple of grunts in acknowledgment and we all set out for our celebratory meal.

Halfway there Dad becomes exasperated. It's probably his knee. He pops two Tums. "That's it. I'm going home."

He turns and walks off. I run after him. "Dad, you can't leave. You have the car. How'll Mom get home? You really want her on a train by herself on Christmas?"

The image of my abandoned atheist Jewish mother on Christmas strikes me as funny but I know I mustn't chuckle.

He stands there for a minute and I imagine steam shooting out of his ears. Poor Dad. He shakes his head, "Come on. Where is this place? I thought you said it was close."

We've walked only three blocks.

I smile at him, but he keeps his mad face on.

We get to the empty restaurant and eat in silence. It takes every bit of my self-control not to poke their eyes out with my fork.

Six months later Mom sends an e-mail. "Wasn't that fun on Christmas? Want to do it again this year?"

I burst out laughing at how nuts they are. Then I'm weeping for how much I love them anyway. I press autodial—1: therapist.

Goodwill to Men

By Sonja Herbert

"**I**s Dad coming for Christmas?" asked eight-year-old Marit.

I looked up from my Spanish textbook, my mind focused on verb conjugations. Before I could make the switch from Spanish to Christmas, Marit's fourteen-year-old sister Marja piped in.

"Yeah, what are we doing for Christmas?" she asked.

"I don't want Dad to be all alone with Judy," eleven-year-old Daniel said.

I felt overwhelmed with the onslaught of my children's questions. I hadn't had time to think about Christmas while studying for my college finals.

Before I could answer, the oldest, Dennis, made a suggestion. "I talked to Dad last weekend. He and Judy are going to Grandma's. Why don't we go too? Then it will be just like last year, and we'll all be together there."

"Gramma, Gramma," my two youngest daughters chanted from the girls' bedroom where I had sent them to put on their pajamas.

"Let me think about it," I said. "Right now I need to study.

We'll talk about it on Friday, after my last exam, okay?"

"Going to Grandma's is a great idea," Marja insisted.

"We'll talk about it later. Now, would you please get Meagan and Liesel to bed while I finish this?"

Grumbling, Marja went off to the bedroom while the other children turned their attention back to the TV. I looked at my Spanish verbs, closed my eyes, and tried to recall the different forms, but now my mind refused to stay focused; thoughts about Christmas tumbled in my head. I closed the book. I would study tomorrow morning, before the test. I sent the children to bed, cleaned up the kitchen, and went to bed myself, still thinking about Christmas.

It would be a terrible holiday, whatever I decided. We could stay here in Utah, me and the six children. Or I could send them all to Colorado to celebrate with their father and his new bride at his mother's house. That seemed like the best solution for them, but what about me? When I married Gary, I had left my home and country to be with him in America. My family stayed behind in Germany. I didn't have the means to go and see them, and even if I did, I would not want to travel without my children. After my divorce, I moved to this small university town and made a good friend, but she was going to California over the holidays. I dreaded the thought of being alone. Without family.

I rolled over in my bed, trying to still my churning mind. Maybe Dennis's idea made sense. I was close to my ex-mother-in-law. We had always gotten along well together, and she stood by my side without judgment when my world fell apart. If we spent Christmas there, I would be with my children and with someone who wasn't just family, but who was also a friend. Her home had three bedrooms, a family room, and a living room—enough space to avoid Gary and his new wife. Maybe for the kid's sake we could be civil.

Two days before Christmas, I packed suitcases for the little ones and me, and supervised the older ones with theirs. We piled into our Ford hatchback and made the trip from Utah to Grandma Towne's home in Colorado.

When we arrived, Gary and Judy were already there. They focused their attention on the children and I stayed close to Grandma in the kitchen, helping her with the stew and biscuits. But in spite of my outer calm, resentment seethed in my chest. Here he was, the winner. He came out of the divorce having the best of both worlds, his children only on weekends and holidays, his new bride, and even his mother. And what did I have? All the work, very little support, and no relief.

The next day Gary and Judy took the kids Christmas shopping and I had time alone with Grandma.

"Are you all right?" she asked.

"It's not the most wonderful Christmas I ever had, Mom," I answered. "I can't help thinking about all the good Christmases we had here when we were a happy family."

"I can only imagine how hard that is. But you're doing great. Just watch the faces of the children. They are so glad that everybody is here and nobody is fighting."

Grandma was right. For the children's sake I would try to stay as nice as I could to my ex. No one would know what I really felt, deep down in my heart.

The night before Christmas, I tucked the kids into their sleeping bags in Grandma's living room, and retired to the same small bedroom Gary and I had shared over the years on our visits. My resentment was like poison. I had no Christmas spirit and didn't want to forgive, least of all to forget.

The next morning, I helped the kids put away their sleeping bags so they could find their presents and open them. Grandma sat in her easy chair; Gary and Judy appeared in their bathrobes and sat on the sofa. I found a place on the loveseat, while the children hunkered down on the carpet.

Amid exclamations of excitement and thanks, the kids opened their packages. As I saw the love and happiness on their faces, something happened in my heart. My resentment receded.

I glanced at Gary. He caught my eye, smiled, nodded.

"Merry Christmas," I ventured with a tentative, shaky smile of my own.

I acknowledged inwardly that, yes, many holidays in earlier years had been good; however, the last few hadn't. And now it all was gone; it was time to move forward.

Today was a new beginning.

Grandma held out a box to me, wrapped in gold and red paper and topped by a bright green bow. Her loving acceptance enveloped me. The heat of the flickering flames in the coal stove added to the warmth in my heart. I was loved. I had a family, right here. Like all families, ours wasn't perfect, but I could live with that.

Gary and I had our differences, and it was a terrible thing that the marriage had to end, but we would go on, linked by love for

Grandma and our six children. I realized that, eventually, I might feel a new love for the father of my children, even though it would never again be the kind we once shared.

With a newfound peace in my heart, I opened my presents, grateful for the unexpected healing this Christmas brought me.

Christmas in Germany: The Naked Truth

By Lori Hein

Santa's a cool guy, and if you ask him to bring your kids' presents a few days early so you can fly to Europe and experience Christmas in Germany, he delivers. Three hours after Dana and Adam opened their gifts and marveled that Santa would make a special trip to Boston just for them, we were headed to the airport and our flight to Frankfurt.

Ah, what a Christmas! Eating cheese-fondued potatoes in Feuchtwangen and sugarcoated snowball cookies in Rothenburg. Sipping mugs of mulled wine while walking cobbled Dinkels-buehl. Singing "Stille Nacht" in a great stone church, strolling outdoor Christmas markets, and browsing festive ornament shops in Heidelberg and Wiesbaden. And in Würzburg, the first town on our itinerary, we experienced German spa life, which includes lots of dunking. And nudity.

Our Würzburg hotel had a *Schwimmbad*—a swim and fitness center—and we couldn't wait to drop our bags and get down there. As we signed in with the girl at the reception desk, I looked through the window behind her at the pool, a sumptuous haven with a waterfall and tropical plants, some dressed for the season in colored holiday lights. Behind one of them stood a buck-naked old man.

I turned to the kids and reminded them—they'd seen topless women on Mediterranean beaches since they were toddlers—that people do things differently in Europe: "You might see a bare body or two in the pool."

My husband, Mike, had a cold and wasn't swimming. He claimed a lounge chair and promptly fell asleep. The kids and I found the single dressing room, a unisex affair. Oblivious to the preponderant nakedness, eleven-year-old Adam climbed into his board shorts and eight-year-old Dana into her neon-pink suit festooned with 101 Dalmatians. Wary, but hopeful we'd simply stumbled into the locker room during a naturist group's annual Christmas get-together, I pulled on my suit and led the kids to the pool.

As the warm water and exercise got our juices flowing, our senses sharpened and we all saw what we'd jumped into. You could have knocked me over with a Speedo when I realized that we three wore the only bathing suits in the whole cedar-planked place.

Taking it in stride, we watched our fellow bathers do "the circuit." They burst from the pool, then ambled, flesh flapping, from sauna to steam to tanning bed to *Frischluft*, or fresh air, an outdoor concrete courtyard with paintings of palm trees, where they sat chatting in fifteen-degrees Fahrenheit in nothing but their *Geburtstag* suits. We caught the hang of the circuit and began to participate in the series of refreshing events.

And that's when we got into trouble.

One man had deputized himself as the pool police and watched our every clothed move. As we'd soon learn, we'd violated the shower-between-events protocol. The enforcer, sometimes swathed in a red and white-striped robe that made him look like a terrycloth candy cane, reported us to the girl at the reception desk who chastised us. After the dressing down, we gave up doing the circuit because all those mandatory showers took too much effort.

Instead, we swam some more, then went to the sauna to cap off our visit. And there awaited the *Schwimmbad* sheriff again. When we sat down, he got up and headed for the front desk. A minute later the receptionist tracked me down and said there "had been complaints" that we hadn't sat on towels while in the sauna.

My tired brain, still operating on eastern standard time, called up the best German it could muster, and I delivered a rough equivalent of, "You're kidding! *We're* wearing clothes! *We're* the hygienic ones! Please tell peppermint-robe-guy that, in the spirit of Christmas, he should keep his parts and his opinions to himself!" (I was pleased with this sudden burst of fluency. Evidently jet lag lets you speak in tongues.) The receptionist apologized and invited the kids to help themselves to a bowl of oranges at the counter.

We woke Mike, still dreaming deeply in his chaise. He'd been oblivious to the naked people lounging and walking near him, and he'd missed the drama. Through it all he'd dozed, the most clothed person this pool had ever seen, his head cold seeking solace beneath long pants, a turtleneck shirt, and a sweater.

But he was barefoot.

"Where are your shoes?" I asked.

"Over there. Some guy in a candy cane robe ordered me to take them off."

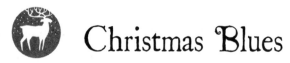

Christmas Blues

By Kathe Campbell

Married children often juggle parents at Christmas.

I call it the every-other-holiday syndrome. Wife's parents on odd years; husband's family on even years. Simple—until unforeseen circumstances found this unsuspecting mom and pop facing a lonely Christmas for the first time. We were not looking forward to the holidays.

We can handle it; we're grownups and we understand. It's okay, we kept reminding ourselves. Okay, that is, until our golden retriever collapsed under a massive seizure that forced us to say good-bye to our beloved lady. We were heartsick over the loss of Nikki.

Oh, dear God, I lamented, *why at Christmastime?* I cried buckets while Ken labored to keep his macho image intact. Finally, he let go and it was a dreadful scene.

A week later, severe arthritis and profound loneliness for Nikki rendered our fifteen-year-old border collie withdrawn, incontinent, and unable to walk. Ginger was what we mountain folks call a dump-off, and we had gladly adopted this sweet and loyal herder. The excruciating final trip to the veterinarian was nearly more than we could handle.

Was celebration of our Lord's birth taking a backseat to our losses?

The morning of Christmas Eve, Ken popped out of bed full of oats and vinegar. I, on the other hand, was still caught up in gloom over beloved dogs and slightly miffed at his attitude.

"I'll be back in a while, dear," he shouted on his way out the door.

The rising sun's pink radiance surfaced the top of our mountain, but our house was deathly still. I stood at the window, pulling myself together and yearning for the holiday-charged din of impatient grandchildren around me.

At noon, Ken returned through the front gate and opened the truck door. Out flew a great tricolored mass of fur.

What on earth?

The ten-month-old keeshond, a Dutch barge dog from the humane shelter, raced through the snow into my outstretched arms. As if we had been bosom buddies forever, we fell over in a joyous heap of emotion, this medium-sized, wiggle-tailed bundle of yips and slurps. "She was the sorriest-looking pup in the place," Ken admitted, "with her brown eyes pleading, 'Please Mister, take me home with you.'" Obviously, Ken was smitten, too.

Villous curly tail dancing a jig atop her back, Keesha snuffled out all the interesting scents on our ranch. She rolled and played in the snow, acquainted herself with kitties, donkeys, ducks, and geese. Thankfully, she had no desire to chase, bite, or torment. She was a keeper.

We took the pup to town for a lovely Christmas Eve dinner (Keesha's came packaged as a doggy box) and then to the pet shop for toys and collar. But Keesha readily averted her nose from silly toys. That night, the thoroughly content, tousle-haired pup held down our big feather bed as we watched yuletide television services between our toes.

Christmas morning arrived with our voices ringing joyful anticipations of the day during phone calls from excited grandchildren across the miles. Instead of hanging around pretending we weren't sadly devoid of family, Ken and I grabbed our new pup and headed for the Salvation Army Church headquarters.

Captain Miss B. welcomed all three of us as I set out table decorations and Ken knuckled down to peel spuds. Frightened she might be abandoned again, Keesha sat as quietly as a mouse in the vestibule, eyeing us with trepidation while Miss B's schnauzer jumped in circles.

More volunteers arrived to serve ham and turkey dinners in an overflowing dining room, a place where humble families and destitute homeless dined in the shadow of Jesus's house. A place where both Ken and I rose above our holiday blues, savoring the meaning of the day as never before.

That night we three wearily returned through our front gate to the echoes of waterfowl and hee-haws lamenting their belated holiday fare. But it was a good tired, our most blessed Christmas ever. Family, we had discovered, could be created.

From both man and beast.

The Tree That Ryma Built

By Ryma Shohami

I was almost five the year my father brought home a fragile Christmas tree ornament. The crimson, snow-roofed Hansel and Gretel cottage proved so irresistible, I almost broke it before it had a chance to make its debut. After that, my hands remained firmly clasped behind my back whenever I was in the vicinity of the tree.

Two years later, in 1957, we emigrated to Poland. We left the Soviet Union, where my father had fled at age sixteen, slightly ahead of the German army that annihilated his village. Now the Soviet authorities finally granted his request to return to his homeland, although our ultimate goal was Canada, where my grandfather had gone before the war to earn money and bring his family to safety. Unfortunately, he had run out of time; my father had been his only child to survive in Grandfather's absence.

Luckily, Poland was providing those with immediate family abroad a brief window of opportunity for emigration. So, while my grandfather was frantically processing our visas, we lived in limbo.

I, of course, was oblivious to our tenuous position. I barely noticed the hushed whispering between my parents; grown-ups were always whispering secrets behind kids' backs. All I knew was that the New Year was fast approaching and no one had yet brought home a tree.

How could I suspect that Christmas tree ornaments were the last thing on my parents' minds?

When I could wait no longer, I nagged my older brother.

"We're not allowed to have a tree anymore," he informed me.

"You're lying," I accused hotly. "We always have a tree!"

"Well, that was Russia, this is Poland, and we can't have a tree. You're so dumb, Ryma. Don't you know Jews aren't allowed to have trees?" he taunted.

What was he talking about? What were Jews? And why couldn't Father Frost come to Poland? My head swirled with all this new information.

Sobbing, I sought reassurance from my parents that the tree would be erected as usual, with its shimmering silver star and the tempting Hansel and Gretel cottage. My father gently explained that in Russia the tree was part of the winter New Year celebrations, just a fun holiday for children, but that everywhere else it symbolized Christmas, a holiday for people who were Christians. We were indeed Jewish and Christmas was not our holiday.

He omitted telling me that in Communist Russia, not having a "New Year" tree would have branded us as Jews, and so we had joined in the festivities.

"But as soon as we're safely in Canada," my mother added, "we'll celebrate our own holidays."

I listened intently, but all I heard was betrayal: *There would be no tree*. I didn't want new holidays; I wanted my tree. I wanted my little house ornament! I was inconsolable.

Refusing to accept their pronouncements, I pocketed the few coins I possessed and went shopping for a tree. The filthy streets were usually overrun by rats, but I had a mission and I would not be intimidated or deterred.

There had been no snow for weeks and the world was a slate gray. The wind whipped me around as I struggled to reach the lot where I had seen our neighbors buying trees. Cold stung my face, adding injury to serious insult.

The lot displayed two leftover scraggly pines, but I didn't care. Any tree would do. Unfortunately, my paltry sum was not enough for even those pathetic specimens.

Hunched with misery, I trudged home. Too proud to be caught crying like a baby, I struggled with the tears scorching my cheeks, pretending they were the result of the dust the wind whipped up.

A block from home, I suddenly noticed that the sidewalks were littered with branches that had broken off the lush trees people had dragged along. I dashed around collecting all the branches I could carry. If I couldn't buy a tree, I would build one!

Staggering under the weight of my accumulation, I finally managed to tumble into the house, where I immediately set about tying together branches into the shape of a tree.

My father scolded, but my mother silenced him with a look and watched with amusement as I cobbled together something whose resemblance to a tree was purely accidental. With ingenuity and my brother's help, I finally succeeded in propping up the bizarre structure.

Next, I crafted a paper star and attached it to the peak. A few smaller versions filled in more spaces, while my red hair ribbons added much-needed festive color to the remaining twigs. Thrilled with my creation, I nevertheless ached for the one ornament that would have completed it.

"Isn't something missing, Ryma?" my mother whispered.

And there was the familiar red house dangling from her finger. She held out the toy and inclined her head toward the tree. I hesitated and glanced at my father. He scowled in disapproval.

"I couldn't just leave it behind," my mother protested.

After what seemed like aeons, my father threw up his hands in exasperated surrender. "I don't want to hear about this once we're in Canada," he warned.

"Go ahead," my mother urged me.

With trembling fingers, I hung the little cottage in its usual place of honor. I had my centerpiece. The tree was now perfect.

In the ensuing years, I have come to appreciate and love the meaningful traditions of the Jewish holidays my family now celebrates. Hanukkah is my favorite. Lighting candles every evening for eight days encourages introspection, while the joyous songs and games provide an opportunity for familial closeness.

But there's another reason I so love this festival of lights—it just happens to fall near Christmas.

Glad Tidings of Great Joy: Heartfelt and Holy Moments

Drawing Names

By Nancy Edwards Johnson

Chilling winds swept down the Blue Ridge Mountains, frosting windows behind the holly sprigs Mrs. Horton had arranged in our first grade classroom. She finished decorating and turned to us. "Kids, Christmas is coming soon. Who wants to draw names?"

"Me! Me! Me!" rang out while hands shot up.

Even Alfred raised his hand. Alfred, who wore dirty, ragged overalls to school although the other boys wore jeans. Miss Horton had told us his mother was sick and asked everybody to be nice to him.

"Aw, Alfred, you won't get to draw names," said Helen.

Mrs. Horton clapped her hands firmly and frowned. "Shhhh, Helen. That's enough. Now everyone get your permission slips signed so you can draw. We'll set a limit of fifty cents."

Not used to being scolded, Helen dropped her head until her long golden hair, so pretty even the teachers talked about it, covered her face.

The bell rang. Brenda snatched the white fuzzy cap with its rabbit-fur pom-poms from my head. "You can wear it again tomorrow," she promised.

The teacher turned to me. "Honey, wearing that cap all day and then taking it off to go outside makes the bitter cold hurt worse."

"That's okay, Miss Horton. When I get off the bus, I wear my headscarf the rest of the way home." My grandma had given me a frayed silk scarf I carried in my coat pocket. Besides, wearing Brenda's cap all day made it worth the extra chill. It was even worth putting up with Alfred.

Alfred used to sit behind Helen, pulling her hair with his grubby hands. When she complained to the teacher, Mrs. Horton asked me to trade seats with Helen. So now Alfred pulled the pom-poms that dangled down the back of my head. Though I hated his teasing, I didn't complain. Instead, Brenda noticed and swapped seats with me.

My excitement built at the idea of drawing names as the school bus bumped down the washboard road and screeched to a halt in front of the little country store. I rushed up the aisle and awaited my turn to hop down the steps. I crossed the road with nary a thought of anything except getting home. Even the chilling winds blasting down the face of Fancy Gap Mountain didn't slow me down.

By the time I ran the half mile home and pushed through the weathered wood door of our two-room farmhouse, I was struggling for breath. Mama pulled me close to the potbellied stove and stoked logs until the fire roared to life. "Now tell me what your hurry's about."

She looked doubtful when I told her about drawing names. "How much are you supposed to spend?"

"Just fifty cents, Mama, and I'll get a present, too."

My excitement at the prospect must have glowed brighter than my chapped cheeks, because Mama's eyes never left my face. Even at six years old, I knew she was thinking how hard fifty cents came.

"Maybe we can figure something out," she finally said. "Just remember, though. You might give something good and get nothing much in return."

I was willing to take the chance. I couldn't wait to draw names.

Next morning Mrs. Horton put slips of paper in a bag and told each of us to pull one out. "Don't tell anyone but me whose name you got. I'll make a list in case anyone forgets. You keep it a secret."

But not everyone did.

"Whose name you got, Alfred?" someone asked.

"Helen's," he sang out with a grin. Helen crinkled her nose.

The last morning of school before holiday vacation, the air on the bus had an electric buzz. Every hand held a present. I'd gotten lucky. Grandma had brought us two boxes of chocolate-covered cherries. Mama let us eat from one box but saved the other for my gift exchange. Alfred clutched a battered package, paper dirty and torn.

One by one, Mrs. Horton distributed presents according to the list on her desk. When she picked up Alfred's torn package, she had the attention of every child in the room. In her other hand, she held a soft-looking package wrapped in bright tissue paper and yarn.

Mrs. Horton walked toward me and paused. I waited, half expecting Alfred's present. Instead, she held out her other hand. I reached for the package and squeezed. It felt as furry as a fuzzy cap!

Then Mrs. Horton stopped in front of Helen's desk. At first Helen drew back like she wouldn't take Albert's gift, but she finally held out her hand.

She ripped the torn paper away to expose an old battered doll, a mop-headed imitation of Raggedy Ann. I remembered seeing the same doll at the beginning of school. Alfred's sister had carried it around, crying and hugging it under her chin. It was dirty and ragged even then.

Helen stared at the doll for the longest time. Then her face crumpled and tears streamed down her chin.

Alfred looked like he'd been slapped. He blinked rapidly.

Mrs. Horton reached over to me, "Honey, would you trade presents with Helen?"

I hesitated a long minute before I grudgingly held out my unwrapped gift to Helen. Brenda slipped under the teacher's arm. "Please, Mrs. Horton, let her keep it. I brought that gift. Helen has no need for it. She already has one like it."

Brenda offered Helen the nicely wrapped exchange present she hadn't yet opened and reached for the doll. She hugged it tightly under her chin.

Alfred let out a sigh I could almost feel. A smile tickled the corners of his mouth and quickly spread into a grin.

I hurried home that evening, loving the way the furry pom-poms of my brand new hat tickled as they swung in the wind. I told Mama how I almost lost it for the dirty Raggedy Ann. "Mama, Alfred's sister really loved that doll."

"Yes, but she loves Alfred, too. When he didn't have anything else to give, she let him take the doll."

"But why did Brenda want it?"

"I don't suspect she really did." Mama slipped an arm around my shoulders and gave me a squeeze. "But, young as she is, Brenda truly knows a gift from the heart when she sees one."

Unto You a Child Is Born

By Helen Colella

"This year," I announced, "Andy will attend Christmas service with us instead of going to the nursery." Some family members murmured that he wasn't old enough. Not old enough to understand the solemnity of the occasion. Not old enough to grasp the meaning of the occasion. Not old enough to sit still.

But I felt that my five-year-old son was ready. "He's going," I insisted.

When he entered St. Peter's Church, Andy pointed. "Look, Dad, green wreaths, like the ones at our house."

We made our way down the aisle.

"Look, Mom, red Christmas flowers like the ones at our house."

Because I didn't want him to miss anything, we slid onto the front row pew. Andy immediately spotted the life-sized Nativity scene at the altar.

"Wow, a big manger, almost like the one at our house."

Shimmering candles cast a warm, calming glow throughout the service. Andy quietly sat and listened to the story of the Nativity, to the angelic voices of the choir, and to enthusiastic parishioners singing the Christmas hymns.

So far so good, I thought, impressed when my son even seemed to listen to the priest. After the final blessing, Andy asked if we could get closer to the altar.

He studied the holy scene and pointed. "There's Baby Jesus in the manger. And there's Mary and Joseph kneeling next to him." Then he named each animal in the stable. He mooed like a cow, baaed like a sheep, bleated like a camel. He even brayed like a donkey. His sound effects were crisp, clear—and loud enough to elicit the grins of others who lingered.

Andy pointed again at the figures. "Three wise men with gifts for Baby Jesus."

I nodded. "Did you like being at the 'big people' service?"

"I liked it fine, but . . ." A small frown pinched his brows.

"What's wrong?"

"Why didn't anyone wish Jesus happy birthday?"

"Would you like to do that?" Dad asked.

Andy nodded and leaned toward the crèche. "Happy birthday," he called out.

Before anyone could comment, he looked at me and frowned a second time. "What's wrong, now?" I asked.

"Why didn't the choir sing the birthday song?"

"Well," his dad questioned, "would you like to do that, too?"

Andy nodded and sang "Happy birthday to you, happy birthday to you" as loud as his young voice could project. When he finished, his smile widened in total satisfaction. Andy beamed at the sudden spurt of applause from those who had gathered around the manger scene, drawn by his sincere performance.

Obviously pleased with the attention—and just as obviously uninhibited—free-spirited Andy turned to the growing crowd at the altar. He opened his arms, extended palm up, praise-fashion, and asked, "Why don't we all sing the birthday song?"

Who could refuse an invitation like that on Christmas Day?

Enthusiastic voices soon filled St. Peter's Church, lifted in a jubilant rendition of the familiar children's song. By the pure joy on Andy's face, I knew my young son did, indeed, understand the true meaning of the occasion. And, with innocent simplicity, he managed to remind us all as we celebrated that Christmas Day.

"Happy birthday, Baby Jesus. Happy birthday to you."

 For ways to remember the true reason for the season, see page 195.

The Red Bike

By J. Vincent Dugas

It was a typical Christmas Eve afternoon. Lines of traffic jammed the mall parking lots, cars vying for spaces close to the building. I had finished all my family shopping and it was still early. I decided to wander the huge toy department and enjoy the childhood memories I always found there.

After browsing aisles, making mental judgments on how toys in my day seemed so much better and more exciting than modern plastic ones, I found myself amid an array of bicycles. I slowed my pace.

There were bikes of all sizes, colors, and types. Some had conventional pedals, some had derailleurs, and others had even more sophisticated gearing devices. As I ran my fingers along the shiny painted surfaces of those magic vehicles, my thoughts skidded to the memory of my first bike.

I smiled a bit, thinking back to the day when my dad walked the little red bike across the road from the bicycle shop where he'd gone to use a phone. Dad had tricked me; he hadn't needed a phone. He went in to buy the bike—a twenty-four-incher with an electric horn. It was the most beautiful thing I ever saw.

I remembered how the horn battery dislodged from its clip every time I hit a bump and laughed out loud as I thought of my adventures on that magic little bike. It was a long time ago, but I recalled how hard my dad worked for the twenty-two dollars needed to buy the two-wheeler.

I stopped to examine one that looked just like mine. Red and shiny, it had balloon tires and an electric horn. *Wow!* I thought. *I could buy this bike now and take it home just for the pleasure of looking at it.* I bent down to read the price tag: ninety-nine dollars. *Not a bad price even sixty-five years later!*

Laughing to myself, I turned to continue my stroll through the store and nearly bumped into a little kid. The boy's huge brown eyes ogled the red bike. I paused when I saw something else in his eyes, something that told another story. They held more than a child's desire for a new possession. They held the knowledge he'd never have a bike like that, but that it surely couldn't hurt to look, to . . . imagine. And in that young boy's imagination was a world of wonder.

My eyes shifted to the mother who stood behind the boy. She looked at her son, her moist eyes apologetic. I knew she could not afford to buy him the bike, and she knew he would not ask for it.

The boy reached out and caressed the red paint. He sucked in a big breath of air, held it, and swallowed, then turned and smiled at his mom. "Okay, Mom," his voice quivered, "we can go now."

His mother slipped an arm around her son and hugged him to her.

Suddenly, someone called out. The voice sounded so familiar to me, and I quickly realized—it was my own.

"Son, would you like to have that bike?" I heard myself say. But the words didn't sound like mine; they sounded more like my father's. "Would you like that bike for your very own? Well, you've got it, son. It's yours. Merry Christmas!" I put my hand on the boy's shoulder. "Just remember, when you're older and able, buy some other kid a bike."

I signaled the floor salesman to prepare the bike. After I paid for it, I walked away and out the door. My own emotions felt visible, like I was wearing them on the outside. After all, I had just had an encounter with my own father; I'd found him within myself.

"Thanks, Dad," I whispered, "for showing me exactly what to do. And thanks again, too, for my own red bike."

Drawn to the Warmth

By Carol McAdoo Rehme

My longtime friend and neighbor Lois is eighty-five. Eighty-five years young, that is. And she's always busy. Painting the interior of her house, weeding her garden, crocheting gifts for her large, extended family—and quilting.

"Well, not really quilting," she says. "I search tag sales all summer long for yard goods and scrap batting and skeins of yarn. Then I cut them to size, bind the edges, and tie them in time for Christmas."

But, as she's quick to point out, they aren't even really quilts. She's selected a smaller version to make. "Lap robes" Lois calls them.

"Big enough to warm arthritic limbs, small enough not to tangle in the spokes of wheelchairs." Lois smiles as she hands me this week's supply. "They're the perfect size for the old folks in the nursing homes."

That's who this spry octogenarian sews for, the *old* folks.

"What, only ten this time?" I tease as I admire the cheery patterns. "Are you slowing down or just getting lazy?"

"Oh, but I've got four dozen cut out and ready to put together," she twinkles back. "They need to be done and delivered by

Christmas. I'll have more for you on Monday."

And I know she will; she always does.

Smiling, I remind her that the staff members will want to know her name so they can send her thank-you notes.

"No." Lois shakes her head in firm rejection of the idea. "This is just between me and God." She points at one of the gift tags she always secures to a bound edge with a strand of bright yarn. Today's card is a picture of Christ in flowing robes, with his hands outstretched. "Just between me and God, to bring a little warmth."

I take the fleece lap robes and my bag of piano music to the holiday sing-along. This one is at the Berthoud Living Center, only ten miles away.

"More quilts," I chant to the activity director. She reaches for them with an eagerness I've come to expect: each area facility admires Lois's handiwork and contributions and disperses them where they are most needed.

"Let's take this one to Lucille." The activity director pulls one from the middle, printed with dainty holly berries and slender candy canes. Lois had tied the fabric with cheery red yarn. "I hope this helps."

"Is Lucille a new resident?"

"Going on two weeks now. She arrived worrying and complaining—and hasn't stopped since. According to her, the expense is 'bothersome' and it's too cold here, 'always too cold.' Lucille just can't seem to get warm." She gives a mighty sigh and her voice softens. "I just wish we could make the transition easier for her, help her settle in. It's hard for her, being away from home at Christmastime." She turns briskly into the hallway. "Maybe this will help."

We walk toward a room halfway down the west-wing corridor.

"Lucille. Lucille?" We raise our voices and rap firmly at her open door to announce our presence. "Look what we have for you."

The ninety-six-year-old perches in her wheelchair like a tiny wren. She turns her head away and refuses to acknowledge us. "It's cold in here," she complains to the wall. "It's cold in here and I can't get warm."

"Lucille, just look. We brought something special." I spread the small lap robe on the bed near her side. "It's a quilt. For you."

"For . . . me?" Her voice is as wrinkled as her face.

"Yes, for you." I grin into her eyes. "Merry Christmas!"

After a lengthy, doubtful pause, she looks up and asks peevishly, "How much will it cost me?"

"Nothing," I assure her. "It's free, a gift. A woman named Lois made it just for you. For Christmas."

"A gift? You're sure it's not going to cost?" Lucille stretches a trembling palm to brush across the yarn's fluff and eyes me uncertainly. "For . . . me?" I nod. And, with a tenderness belying her querulous attitude, she runs a bent finger across the small card Lois had attached to the quilt.

Her ridged, yellowed fingernail inches along. First, Lucille traces Christ's white robe, next his gentle face, and, at last, his outstretched arms. The full length of one, then the entire length of the other.

And she sighs from the depths of her heart as she draws the soft Christmas quilt to her cheek. "*Now,* I'm warm. For the first time since coming here, I finally feel warm."

Thanks to Lois and her pact with God.

Yuletide in the Tropics

By Connie Alexander Huddleston

"I t's a shame we don't know someone else to help eat this food," I said to my husband, as I attempted to squeeze a tropical fruit salad into the overflowing refrigerator.

In a little more than an hour, we would share our Christmas Eve dinner with a family that worked with us at Hogar Misionero, a school for missionaries' children in Panama. Another missionary family that lived in the Darien jungle and worked with the Kuna tribe would join us, too.

But our neighbors had their own celebrations planned, and the rest of the school staff had gone interior to celebrate with mission families staying at their jungle stations during the holidays.

"It would be nice to have more guests for dinner," my husband agreed, "but I don't know who else we could invite on such short notice. I'm just glad the Simmons and Horvats can come."

"So am I. Between our three families, we'll have enough youngsters to act out the Christmas story tonight."

With the food preparation done, I began decorating the dining table. I used artificial evergreen branches paired with fresh red hibiscus from our yard. Like many parts of our celebration since we had come to Panama, the centerpiece was a mixture of the traditional and the tropical.

An artificial tree we brought from the United States stood in front of an open window through which the warm breezes of the dry season blew. The tree was festooned in glass bulbs and plastic snowflakes, but its branches also held straw stars woven by the women of the Choco tribe and appliquéd fish and birds that were needlework creations of the Kunas.

As I placed the last flower in the arrangement, I heard someone calling at the gate.

"Hello, Brian, you're early," I greeted. "Where's the rest of your family?"

"Oh, I'm here to let you know we can't make it tonight," Brian said. "A family from our Kuna village came to visit; we don't think we should show up to dinner with five extra people."

"Bring them! We have plenty of food. Harry and I were just wishing there was someone else to invite."

"Wonderful. The Kuna family told us they wanted to see how Americans celebrate one of their festivals."

"Since we plan to exchange gifts this evening, I'll do some quick shopping for them," I offered.

After Brian gave me the rundown on the family, I told Harry about the change in plans and headed for the store. It was a small grocery, but it also carried a selection of dry goods and miscellaneous supplies.

I quickly chose a set of towels for the mother and a new machete for the dad. I knew barrettes and a couple of small dolls would delight the little girls, and I selected small shirts for the baby boy. Some fruit-flavored hard candies completed our gifts to them. I hurried home and finished wrapping just as the first guests arrived.

We began our celebration with dinner. Because we knew they, like many people, would be tentative about trying new foods, we explained to them that the baked ham was like *macho monte*, a wild pig they eat. They took large portions. They recognized rice and the pineapple and coconut salad and added them to their plates. They all turned down the Jell-O though; when they saw it wiggling, we couldn't convince them it wasn't alive. However, we had no trouble enticing them to try our *dulces* (sweet desserts). They even came back for seconds.

English, Spanish, and Kuna swirled around as we sought to communicate across cultures in whichever languages we knew. Although the dad spoke some Spanish, the Kuna family spoke no English. It helped that the Simmons spoke fluent Kuna because the rest of us knew Spanish but only a smattering of Kuna.

As I considered our language situation, I wondered what we should do about reading the Christmas story. Though progress was being made, there was not yet a printed version of the New Testament in the dialect of the village where our visitors lived.

"Brian, can you translate as the Christmas story is read and the children act it out?" I asked.

"Yes. It will be a great way to show the reason for our celebration," he replied.

I dressed the American children in bathrobes, sheets, and towels.

The three kings wore cardboard crowns and the shepherd carried a stuffed toy lamb. We gave the Kuna children front-row seats for the play. Tom Horvat read the account of the Savior's birth in English, pausing a verse at a time while Brian translated. We watched as our children mimed the familiar scenes on a makeshift stage.

"And the angel said unto them, 'Fear not,'" Tom read, "'for, behold, I bring you good tidings of great joy, which shall be to all people.'"

I looked at the faces of our unexpected guests. Their eyes filled with wonder as the story of the Lord's birth unfolded before them. I realized that I was seeing a fulfillment of the scripture: a Kuna family—miles and centuries removed from Bethlehem—was hearing, in their own language, the good tidings. They were the "all people" of which the angel spoke. I felt blessed that on Christmas Eve I was seeing that promise fulfilled.

When we reached the end of the story, Brian prayed in Kuna, giving thanks for the gift of the Christ Child and for the presents we were about to exchange. As towels and machetes, barrettes and dolls were opened, it was easy to see that the language of gifts is the same in any culture. Ours said *I want to be your friend.*

The unexpected gift of our multicultural celebration that year, and the years that followed when our Kuna friends returned again, are among my most treasured Christmas memories.

I now celebrate Christmas in the United States, but I still mix the traditional with the tropical. My tree is trimmed with glass balls and plastic snowflakes, Choco straw stars, and Kuna appliqués. Now I see the fulfillment of the angel's announcement in the wonder on my grandchildren's faces when they hear the Nativity story.

But whether shared in English or tribal tongue, in a Midwest town or a tropical rain forest, with friends of diverse cultures or within the family circle, each telling is a continuation of "good tidings . . . to all people."

Bah, Humbug! When Christmas Seems More Blue Than White

The Butterfly Tree

By Jeanne Hill

When the supervisor turned down my Christmas leave request for the third year in a row, she shot me that old saying, "Duty has its own rewards, dear." *Bedpan duty on an obstetrics ward?* I thought. *Not likely.*

That night, the only person on 4-Center worse off than me was Emily, a first-time mother my age who had come in two days ago and delivered a beautiful full-term boy. Stillborn. Poor, pale Emily had not eaten or even slept much since. My heart ached for the frail girl, but none of us could reach her. Seldom speaking, she remained turned to the wall, long taffy hair streaming down her back and IV bottles hovering above her, feeding her through the vein.

Aside from Emily and construction sounds, 4-Center was not a challenge. Due to remodeling, the ward shared a temporary hall wall with a delivery room. During the day, the workmen's amplified hammering was nerve-racking. At night, exaggerated sounds whipped in on the wind, making the place spooky.

The next night, I dreaded going on duty because it was traditional for the night nurse to decorate the ward tree, and hospital decorations were skimpy. As soon as the ward was quiet, I started hanging scuffed red, gold, and silver ornaments on the lopsided pine that listed toward the temporary wall. When I finished, the bedraggled tree looked terrible.

I was shaking my head in despair when I answered Emily's call light. She wanted a blanket and, as I tucked it around her legs, she surprised me with, "What's wrong?"

"I can't get the ward Christmas tree to look decent," I confided. Again she surprised me by asking to be put into a wheelchair for a look at the tree. So I bundled her and her IV bottles into the wheelchair and carefully wheeled her to the tree across from the nurses' station.

She examined my pitiful effort.

"We could make some ornaments," she suggested, her gray eyes showing a faint spark of interest. I admitted that I wasn't any good at that. "I'm not either," she said. "All I know how to make are paper butterflies. I learned how in grade school."

At my questioning look, she explained. "You paste a sheet of red cellophane paper between black paper butterflies whose wings have been cut out for the red to show through. Then you cut trim for the butterflies, pinch them in the middle, and staple their centers to raise the wings. They're pretty."

Butterflies hardly seemed appropriate for a Christmas tree, but since they were the only thing that captured Emily's interest, I agreed. Emily's husband shored up the tree and brought supplies. When I came on duty the next night, a bevy of beautiful butterflies flitted across Emily's dresser.

"Their red cellophane wings shine like ruby-stained glass!" I praised. "I'll cut and paste some tonight between call lights, Emily. Emily?" She was sound asleep.

"Wore herself out making butterflies," the day nurse informed me, "but she actually ate some dinner this evening."

Emily and the tree progressed together. When the first wave of butterflies alighted on the branches, Emily's IV feeding was discontinued. Her color returned and a fragile light flickered in her eyes as she surveyed the beautiful tree swarming with red and black butterflies three days later.

I brought my carved wooden crèche with its wooden Baby Jesus wrapped in red burlap and placed it under the tree. The evergreen and the crèche were all Emily talked about. She sat beside the tree each evening, chatting and smiling wanly at the spooky wind sounds from the temporary wall nearby.

On Christmas Eve, the wind died down, giving way to a quiet snowfall. I was drawing midnight lines on charts, while Emily sat in her wheelchair between the nurses' station and the Christmas tree, when we heard it—a newborn's electrifying cry that pierced the silent night! The cry seemed to come from the crèche under the tree.

Emily and I stared wide-eyed at the burlapped figure of Baby Jesus. The baby's cry pierced the air again. My pen poised midair over a chart. Though I knew the cry had to have come from a newborn in the delivery room, reverberating through that temporary wall near the crèche, it was as if we were hearing the cry of Baby Jesus himself all those years ago.

Emily must have felt the same. The next moment she was out of her chair and running to me, crying and hugging me.

"I've got a duty to him," she said, glancing at the crèche, "as well as to my husband—a duty to get well and get on with my life."

I nodded agreement, delighted to see this new resolve in my patient.

And that's when it hit me: if my Christmas leave request hadn't been denied that year, I would've missed the butterfly tree and the baby's cry that made the season special.

Duty does have its own rewards! I thought.

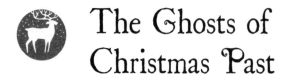

The Ghosts of Christmas Past

By Joseph Hesch

I've been called just about all the evil names connected to Christmas you can think of—Grinch, Scrooge, Party Pooper, you name it. People think I hate Christmas.

They couldn't be more wrong.

I love everything Christmas is about, or is supposed to be about. But my history—and how I've reacted to it—doesn't goose me into outbursts of Yuletide yippees.

When I was a little kid, and more so as a tween and teen, Christmas was always a tough time for my family. Dad was an operating engineer, one of those bulldozer-driving dudes with the year-round farmer's tan and more often than not, no job from Pearl Harbor Day until spring.

I'm not going to tell you that we suffered through bleak Christmases. We always had a decent tree and some presents, but nothing too extravagant or anything in excess. Classmates would come back to school after New Year's crowing about the gifts they'd got. I would mumble about the one cool gift Santa left me. Slippers, pajamas, and stocking stuffers like oranges and Lifesavers didn't count.

We were kind of lucky as young kids because Grandma Short-all had no grandkids to spoil but us. Again, though, Grandma S. wasn't rolling too many bills into a wad herself. One gift, some home-knit mittens, chips and dip, and "see ya!"

On the way home from Christmas Eve at Grandma's house, Dad drove a curlicue route through Albany. It gave those of us who had some awake left a ringside seat at the light show, one that starred all the houses in the soon-to-be run-down neighborhood where Grandma lived, all around town, and through the tony Pine Hills neighborhood where everything was understated and overpriced.

I reclined sideways across the backseat, little brothers Jimmy and Billy propped in hooded-eyed doze against each other at my feet. I could see lights right, left, up, and down, without moving my head. I loved light-looking in that big old Chrysler!

Once home, the Old Man got cranky about how we little buzzards better be getting our bottoms into bed. (That's a bowdlerized quote, by the way. You get the picture.) That's when he would give me religion by repeating the story about him waking up in the middle of one Christmas Eve night and finding that the "right jolly old elf" didn't want any underage sidewalk superintendents spying on his big night's work. Dad said Santa eyeballed him and pulled out his reindeer whip and snapped it across his little keister.

I'd heard this story many times, yet it always gave me pause. While at age seven I was already reading Cooper, Twain, and Melville, I wasn't so sophisticated that I would call the Old Man's bluff and sneak a peek in the parlor after he and Mom turned off the tree lights.

Hence, I slept with my head under the covers. It was warmer, it kept my brother Jimmy from breathing onion dip on me, and—just in case—it kept me on the Nice List.

The following dawn, we kids were up before Mom and Dad, delighted to see that Santa had arrived and none of us had screwed up during the preceding year. Everybody had their own big gift and some little stocking stuffers. I remember getting little cardboard and clear plastic mazes and trying to maneuver a tiny BB from the outer ring to the center and vice versa. Combine the all-family gifts—board games one year, a dartboard another, stuff we all could use—along with what Grandma S. gave us, and Grandma Hesch's knitwear, and we were pretty happy little dudes. Honest.

After we went to Christmas morning Mass with Mom, we'd come back to our flat on Bradford Street and find Dad preparing a ham for baking with brown sugar and ginger ale glaze and pineapple slices and maybe some cherries. We also would see that he had opened his seasonal bottle of Manischewitz, sipping it from either an old piece of cut-glass stemware or a Flintstone jelly jar. Hedrick's beer flowed from brown quart bottles as the day's celebration lengthened and loosened.

Nevertheless, Christmas was great for me as a kid; it's just that I learned not to go overboard about it. We couldn't afford it. And I was okay with that. But lean Christmases were deeply imprinted on me.

Now I wince and shake my head at how my kids are spoiled at Christmas. My wife doesn't think so. Our girls, visiting their affluent, private-school friends, probably don't think so either. Daughter One is the Christmas poster girl. She'd give gifts from

Thanksgiving to Twelfth Night. Daughter Two wants the best, but has enough of my traits in her to not ask. But all three of them never experienced what I think is the true miracle of Christmas.

No. It wasn't anything like a virgin birth, word made flesh, star in the East, God-bless-us-every-one kind of miracle. But it was no less miraculous. It was more of a loaves-and-fishes kind of miracle.

How did an often-unemployed, heavy-equipment jockey and his stay-at-home wife manage to pull off perfectly marvelous, want-for-nothing Christmases for their full quiver of kids? Answer: save what you can, when you can, and learn to say "No" like you mean it.

Dad collected his unemployment check each week of the winter, and Mom saved a few bucks from each of his warm-weather paychecks throughout the rest of the year. We managed and didn't feel deprived. What good would it do to stew over what we didn't or couldn't have? Why not celebrate what we did have?

No, I don't get too excited about Christmas anymore. Probably not like you and yours do. Rather, I get quiet and pensive. But I'm not brooding.

See, I love Christmas because I've felt its spirit and I've seen its miracle. In all honesty, it really doesn't take all that much.

Radio Flyer

By Todd Outcalt

The little red wagon had been a part of our family for three generations. My grandfather pulled it as a child during the dark days of the Depression. My father inherited it in the 1940s and spent a good deal of his early years of childhood using it to haul home groceries and as a go-cart when he found a hill steep enough to rocket him to the bottom.

Eventually the Radio Flyer became my ride, too.

You remember the little red wagon, don't you? Or maybe you still have one—tucked away in the attic, hiding in the shed, stored in the basement behind the stairs, or shoved into a corner of the garage. The little red wagon—the Radio Flyer—has been a part of the American landscape for many years.

Our Radio Flyer was an heirloom, and I decided to pass it along to my first child.

Soon after our daughter was born, my wife and I pondered the possibilities for her first Christmas—a day defined not so much by faith and celebration as by the stark realities of our financial situation. Our condition was made all the more preposterous when we discovered that the Radio Flyer had been stolen from our garage a few days before we planned to put it under the Christmas tree—our first gift to our little girl.

"Who would take a little kid's wagon?" I grumped time and again.

"Let it go," my wife implored.

Of course, I did let it go—eventually. I also let go of more cash than I had intended that year. But as the days passed and we purchased gifts for everyone in the family but our daughter, my thoughts returned again to the promise of a little red wagon under the tree.

"We should just buy her another one," I suggested. "It's the only thing to do."

"We can't afford a wagon," my wife insisted. "Besides, she needs socks and shoes and pajamas. She doesn't need a little red wagon."

My wife was right, of course. Pajamas it would be. Maybe a pair of socks. Perhaps a small stuffed animal for the crib.

Christmas Eve passed, not with visions of sugarplums or a visit from some generous Santa, but with a kind of heaviness in our hearts.

I slept restlessly and woke on Christmas morning with a feeling of heaviness. I needed coffee before I could face the sunshine glinting on a fresh snowfall.

"This could have been a special Christmas," I lamented to my wife as I pushed the covers aside and dragged myself from bed.

Together, the two of us gathered the baby—milky warm and snuggly soft—from her crib. We padded down the short, narrow hallway toward the sad little evergreen we had carved from a hedgerow in the backyard. We eased into the small room, feeling no holiday joy. I slumped onto the couch, still mourning the Christmas-that-should've-been.

Even the tree looked dejected, dried, and wilted in its stand, brown needles littering the carpet. The gifts were as sparse as the branches above them that sagged under the weight of ornaments.

"I wish we had the Radio Fly—" A flash of red caught my eye. Beneath the tree was a shiny red wagon.

"What? How?" I looked at my wife and lifted an eyebrow.

"I found it at the Goodwill store." She grinned when I lifted the baby into my arms and eased next to the Radio Flyer to place her, still sleeping, in the wagon bed.

Using the wagon like a cradle, I gently rolled the wheels back and forth and back and forth.

It was a beautiful sight, baby and wagon, both rosy and bright and easing toward a promising future. My daughter still innocent and so new to her young parents; the used Radio Flyer not unlike the treasured family hand-me-down; my wife and I flush with anticipation and hopeful dreams.

This all happened years ago, but the Radio Flyer now sits in the basement closet anticipating another Christmas, another child.

As my wife and I grow older together, the little red wagon embodies the spirit that beckons us to pass along some part of ourselves to those we love. The gift or the memory could be anything, really—a favorite ornament, a ritual, a poem, a story. What we choose to give is not as important as how we give it. Christmas joy can be created in plenty or in want, so long as love is offered and hearts are open.

But a Radio Flyer doesn't hurt, either.

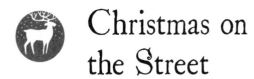

Christmas on the Street

By Pat Mendoza

J aded. That's what I had become. But four years in the navy and five more as a police officer will do that to almost anyone. And Christmas was not my favorite time of year.

In the military, I found it incredulous that strung below a destroyer's five-inch guns in Christmas lights were the words "Peace on Earth." I always felt that it should have included the words "Or Else." To me, it was the ultimate dichotomy.

During the holiday season, police departments all over the country handle the highest rate of suicides and homicides of the year. Our department was no different. Depression and anger were the other great paradoxes in a season celebrating "peace and joy."

It also seemed that every nutcase around came floating up out of the Yuletide. Like Mrs. Rogers, who was convinced aliens were trying to get to her. Comparatively, she was easy to deal with and always made a great batch of chocolate chip cookies for the officer who answered her daily "de-alienation" calls. She may have been crazy, but she knew how to bake.

With each day that passed, I thought I had witnessed everything: riots, homicides, robberies, traffic fatalities, suicides. I'd encountered amazing street people. I'd dealt with odd personalities. But every time I thought I'd seen it all, something would happen that showed me I hadn't seen anything yet.

During Christmas week, two fellow officers I worked with were involved in a fatal shooting during an attempted robbery of a coin store. Hostages were taken, including one officer. Another walked into the situation, and a robber opened fire. I came awfully close to losing two of my brother officers.

Merry Christmas.

Four days later, I received an accident call at around 6:00 PM. Seems Tuna Fish, one of our more colorful and congenial street people, had walked out between two parked cars directly into the path of a teen driver. I got there in time to watch him die. The sixteen-year-old wasn't cited. Even though we told the kid it wasn't his fault, I knew he would live with the memory the rest of his life.

Merry Christmas.

It took me about five hours to clear the accident and deal with the paperwork. The first thing I did when I got back to the station was shower and don a fresh uniform. I went back on patrol half wishing Mrs. Rogers would call about her aliens. Somehow, the thought of chocolate chip cookies seemed obscenely good.

As the night progressed I made a few traffic stops and thought that the end of the shift would find me in a bar frequented by cops, one way to cope during the Christmas season. But just forty minutes before shift change, I got another ambulance call. This was not an accident. It was an emergency medical response and mine was the closest car. I didn't have time to think; my training took over. I was now running siren and red lights.

I arrived at the apartment before the ambulance.

Although Police Academy training had included first aid for

just about anything—compound fractures, bleeders, knife and gunshot wounds—this situation made me sweat. What I found was an expectant mother . . . who wasn't going to wait for any ambulance. I don't know who was more scared, the inexperienced new mother or me. This was our first baby!

I had never assisted or even witnessed a delivery except in the first aid movie they showed at the academy, the movie at which many macho cops lost their cookies. But I did recall what the instructor had said. "Remember: that baby's gonna come whether you want it to or not."

I tried to calm the mother and myself. My mind yelled in sync with her labor pains: *Come on ambulance!* alternating with the prayer, *Please don't come out yet!*

The ambulance didn't make it in time.

During the longest few minutes of my life, the baby emerged, and he was really, really slippery. I gently placed the little guy on his mother's stomach.

As messy as I was, I didn't mind one bit. I had just witnessed a miracle, a tiny new life. More importantly, I witnessed it at Christmas, in the quiet of a one-bedroom apartment—where I truly found some peace on earth.

The ambulance arrived within minutes of the delivery and transported mother and *our* wee Christmas package to the hospital. Both were healthy and doing well.

I did end the night at that bar, but no longer to cope. I lifted my glass in a silent, celebratory toast.

Merry Christmas.

Holidaze

By Diane Perrone

*C*hristmas had always been my favorite season, and I stretched its limits. For me, the countdown began on December 26: "Only 364 shopping days until . . ."—until my divorce.

That year, every horizontal surface in my home, formerly festooned in holiday decor by the day after Thanksgiving, lay bare well into Advent. Hooks on the exterior of the house, usually teeming with hundreds of light strands, held only icicles. No cinnamon wafted from my kitchen. No festooned gifts stashed from children in obscure places. No carols blared from the stereo; it was in my ex's bachelor pad.

After twenty-three years of marriage and a three-month separation, my heart was broken. It certainly wasn't into Christmas.

Winter was as bleak as my mood. Snowless branches stood naked and vulnerable. Severe cold and icy sidewalks imprisoned me. I looked out my picture window, day after day, as numb on the inside as the ground outdoors.

One evening, I noticed our house suddenly ablaze with the light display it always wore this time of year. The next morning,

I stepped on pine needles strewn across the kitchen floor and followed their trail down the basement stairs, through the laundry area, and across the rec room to a seven-foot tree leaning in a stand.

I discovered a frosted German Stollen hidden in the freezer amid frozen chickens. Another day, our Advent wreath mysteriously appeared, complete with recycled candles. Finally, countless boxes of holiday decorations mysteriously made their way from the attic to the living room.

No one in the family discussed a real tree; we all knew we couldn't afford the traditional twelve-footer we usually purchased for the stairwell. And the Charlie Brown tree in the basement, a midnight acquisition by my son's well-meaning friends, was already needleless. Instead, someone located an artificial tree. The branches didn't resemble bottle brushes once they were dripping in ornaments.

What we did discuss was establishing new traditions, not only because the old ones were painful but also because our family dynamics were changing. I told my adult children to celebrate with their loved ones and their families.

All I really wanted to do was attend Midnight Mass; whether they joined me or not was okay. Surprisingly, they all showed up, even those who rarely attended church.

On Christmas morning, my daughter and her new husband appeared at 8:00 AM and put a turkey in the oven before the rest of us woke. We opened gifts in our pajamas and left crumpled wrappings on the floor. Snacks blended into meals as the kids came and went to celebrate with friends and future in-laws.

We laughed some. We cried some. We reminisced a lot. Talking about the past took the sting out of bittersweet memories.

I don't remember all the details of my first Christmas as a single-again woman. But I will always remember that the year I couldn't do Christmas, my children did it for me.

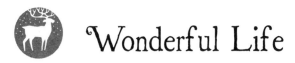

Wonderful Life

By Caroline Grant

It's my first Christmas as a mom. As I sit rocking infant Ben to sleep in the darkened room, I realize the ubiquitous Christmas telecast of *It's a Wonderful Life* is flickering on the hospital's ancient television.

The sound is muted, but I remember the dialogue. George Bailey (Jimmy Stewart) has just learned that Uncle Billy misplaced the day's deposit, and despite sacrificing his whole life for the Building & Loan, George is ruined. He can't listen to his wife Mary cheerfully prattle on about their daughter Zuzu's cold. He rages about money spent on the doctor, their money pit of a drafty house: "I don't know why we don't all have pneumonia!"

Ben stirs in his sleep and cries out. I hold my breath as I adjust his IV, which has tangled around my arm and pulled taut. I touch my lips to his sweaty head and he relaxes back into sleep. I exhale, relieved to avoid a repeat cycle of the anguished cries that raise his fever and bring the nurses running with another round of invasions.

We have pneumonia.

Ben is the only one sick, but as long as he is in the hospital, my husband, Tony, and I might as well have pneumonia, too. We haven't slept or showered in days, and we're subsisting on the cold microwave burritos and donuts Tony bought on his fevered run to the market when we realized we'd be here a while. My sister delivered food at some point, but that's long gone.

I'm aching to nurse Ben, who doesn't have the strength to suck more than a moment or two, so every few hours I submit to the pain and indignity of an industrial-sized pump wheeled from the maternity ward.

Now snow is falling heavily, and we'll have no more visitors until the town plows get to work. Even if Ben were well enough to leave, we would not be able to manage the twisting dirt road back to my parents' house.

Tony and I have come, with my siblings, their spouses, and their kids, to my parents' home in New England. I had imagined Ben tearing wrapping paper and chewing on ribbon; I was ready to keep him from tugging on the dangling bell ornaments and toppling the tree my dad cut from his own small lot; I was looking forward to offering him a fingertip dipped in eggnog, his first gingerbread man, a wedge of Yorkshire pudding.

Instead, we are in a small country hospital with our very sick boy, and I'm jealous of the bankrupt, fictional George Bailey because Zuzu only has a cold.

It's a Wonderful Life is considered a simple and sentimental movie, but there's nothing like watching it in a hospital to see the film's darkness, and it is the frank engagement with life's real worries—from disease to poverty to war—that I admire. The film opens with shots of snowy, bucolic Bedford Falls, but a voice-over reveals people anxiously praying for their friend, husband, and father George Bailey.

We flash back to his childhood, where moments of happiness turn quickly: Sledding with friends, George saves his brother from drowning and is permanently injured as a result. Flirting with a girl at the local soda fountain, George learns that the owner's son has just died in the flu epidemic. When George notices that the grief-stricken pharmacist has filled a prescription incorrectly, we witness his second, but by no means last, act of protective parenting.

He's a parent long before he has children, always putting the needs of others before his own. He wants to travel the world, build important buildings, make an impact; instead, he never leaves his hometown. He takes over his father's business and marries that girl from the soda fountain.

His own children (four in all) arrive in voice-over and don't figure into the story until their ruined father rages about their existence to his puzzled wife: "You call this a happy family? Why do we have to have all these kids?"

It's a shocking, ugly scene. Mary watches him quietly, suggests he leave, then asks their stunned children to pray for him.

It's the most mothering we've seen from Mary (Donna Reed, in the role that cemented her reputation as the perfect movie mom). Until now, she's been quietly industrious, fixing up the house and volunteering in the war effort, the kids playing at her side. Mary is calm, competent, and efficient (who wouldn't be with such unreal children?), but all the while she makes things happen when George despairs. She's the one to buy the couple a house, and at the film's end she takes up a collection to forestall George's bankruptcy.

Meanwhile, George, weary of parenting his entire community, is given a tour of the village—without him in it—to appreciate his impact and importance, to renew his commitment to the town and his family. It's an opportunity parents never get, and we could all use the perspective.

Sitting in that hospital room rocking Ben, my thoughts skate treacherously in the other direction. I start to imagine my world, only recently transformed by my child, without his demanding, amazing presence. Where would I be without him? Surely not in this hospital room, and that thought suddenly makes the antiseptic space seem sweet.

All I can do is hold him, and so that's all I do, hour after hour, until at last, late on Christmas night (or is it early the next morning?), Ben wakes without tears for the first time in days. To my great relief he nurses well and then, miracle of miracles, he smiles at me.

What a wonderful life.

Talking Turkey: Holiday Food and Other Fiascos

Eating at Two

By Robert W. Howe

Each year the same six Wyoming families gather on Christmas for a day of togetherness and turkey with all the trimmings. Most of the time we meet at our ranch, but on this particular year another family hosted the dinner.

Even before the big day, there were signs of trouble, but everyone ignored them. Becky was hostess, although she had, in fact, never cooked a turkey. As the holiday approached, she asked a few questions of the other women and seemed to have it all in hand.

Late Christmas morning, we all arrived at Becky's house. Every family brought their part of the meal—cheeses, special vegetable dishes, candied squash, fixings to make mashed potatoes, green bean casseroles, and half a dozen pies and other desserts.

"What time will the turkey be ready?" someone asked.

"Let's see. I put it in at nine this morning and according to what Loie and Kathy told me, it should take about fifteen minutes per pound." Becky eyed the clock. "So I guess we'll be eating at two."

Everyone went their separate ways to play and socialize. By one o'clock, the potatoes bubbled and the tables gleamed with dishes and flatware. At half past one, Lynn was at the stove, poking the boiling potatoes for doneness and soliloquizing loudly. "I love the snow on the ground, being together, the food filling the table, the smell of turkey baking in the oven. Say—I don't smell the turkey."

He was right. The house was filled with lots of things: laughter, Christmas carols, the murmur of quiet conversations, side dishes sizzling on the range, the bump and thump of kids tousling with their toys, the stomp of boots in the hallway as people returned from sledding or snowshoeing—but not the aroma of turkey.

When Becky opened the oven door, only steam and heat came out, no heavenly scent. Something was definitely wrong. She set the roaster on top of the stove and we leaned closer to look at the royal bird. When she removed the foil, the turkey, surrounded by dry, crisp stuffing, was pale and barely warm—even after four and a half hours of cooking.

"I can't understand it," Becky said. "I took the turkey out of the freezer this morning about eight. It took me about an hour to fix the stuffing, and I put it into a preheated oven by nine."

"Becky, you didn't thaw the turkey?"

"No. Was I supposed to?"

Lynn examined the cavity of the oversized bird. "The giblet bag is still in there, frozen solid." We all laughed as he struggled to pry it loose. When he finally slid the turkey back into the oven, we figured it would be closer to five o'clock before Christmas dinner would be served.

Stomachs rumbled and so did the restless crowd that had emerged by now, lured by hunger and curiosity to the kitchen.

"But I can't wait until five," one of the children whined—or maybe it was one of the dads. After all, we'd been working up an appetite for some time and had returned at the appointed hour ready to eat.

"Why don't we eat the pies?" someone suggested. "You've heard the expression: 'Eat dessert first!'"

"She's right. We never fully savor dessert after a heavy holiday meal. Let's have it first!"

Within a few minutes the elements were spread out. There was an array of ice cream, crackers and cheese, coffee and milk—and the pies. Peach, apple, and berry. French silk. And banana cream.

A meal of pies? The children were delighted (and so were the dads) that moms not only agreed, but piled their helpings high. My own plate held four generous slices, four different flavors, but I did balance it off with a few wedges of cheese.

I looked at the clock. Actually, Becky's prediction was right on the nose: we were eating at two.

Almost three decades later, the same families—those children now bringing spouses and children of their own—gather to celebrate Christmas. We still prepare turkey with all the trimmings, but no one would dream of serving it at midday. Instead, the entire clan swarms around the tables to celebrate a lasting holiday tradition—and eat the pies first.

 If you'd rather eat the turkey first, see page 202 for how to time your feast as well as other must-know turkey tips.

The Right Ingredients

By Robyn Kurth

When Greg and I first moved from Chicago to Orlando, maintaining our Christmas traditions was only a plane ticket away. But three years later, the thought of slogging through an overcrowded airport with our two-year-old son, Alex, while I was nearly eight months pregnant made Christmas in Florida seem like the only sane option.

Even though my in-laws were coming to spend the holidays with us, I privately mourned my losses. There would be no chance to see the enormous Christmas tree in Chicago's Daley Plaza. No stroll down nearby State Street to marvel at Marshall Field's animatronic window displays. No chill in the air to remind me that it was the most wonderful time of the year. I wondered how I could have the Christmas spirit in my heart when the rest of me was a thousand miles away from home.

Earlier that year we had moved from an apartment to a new house, so I had no more excuses for neglecting to pull out the holiday ornaments. We hadn't even bothered setting up the large Christmas tree when we lived in our apartment, especially when we spent most of December "up North," as Floridians like to say.

A hand-me-down from Greg's parents, our artificial tree had color-coded branch ends chipped and faded from Christmases past. The top portion of the tree was bound together with twine and a short, thick wooden stick that protruded like a sore thumb from a torn mitten.

I remembered how my parents passed along an angel tree-topper from my childhood that fit perfectly over the exposed lumber. The angel was an early 1970s dime-store trinket with a plastic doll's head, acrylic blond hair, felt arms that clutched a tiny tinsel halo, and a cardboard body covered with thin golden foil. The angel's golden wings clung to its back with yellowed Scotch tape, yet the tattered relic meant more to me than any expensive ornament ever could.

But where was it? The angel had adorned our inherited tree in the first house Greg and I owned, but I hadn't seen the tree-topper since we moved to Florida.

Although I couldn't reconstruct my favorite Christmas places or replace my missing angel, I was able to recreate my favorite Christmas delicacies: Polish food—hard to locate south of the Mason-Dixon Line. I acquired a few ready-made items at the only Polish deli in town, including several links of smoked kielbasa sausage (shipped all the way from a Chicago meatpacker) and some fresh cheese and potato pierogi dumplings.

The centerpiece of my traditional Polish Christmas dinner would be *golumpki*, as it was called by my Polish maternal grandmother, also called *holubki* by my Slovak paternal grandmother. However you spelled it or attempted to pronounce it, the meat-filled stuffed cabbages (pigs in a blanket) were the highlight of every Christmas dinner I had eaten since I was old enough to digest solid foods.

Just assembling the main ingredients put me in a more festive mood—whole cabbage heads, onions, tomato soup, beef broth, rice, eggs, and ground sirloin. By Christmas Day my pantry was brimming with the fixings for a hearty ethnic meal, and my refrigerator contained the heavenly scent of the kielbasa's smoke flavoring and heavy garlic seasoning. Now that was the smell of Christmas!

However, preparing my authentic Polish Christmas meal turned out to be a five-hour odyssey. My legs throbbed from standing for so long. Worse yet, my unborn daughter pounded inside me with all-too-familiar Braxton Hicks contractions. Yet the tangy aroma of sauce simmering on the stovetop promised I would be richly rewarded for my efforts.

The meal was a resounding success and tasted just as good as I remembered. The tree lights twinkled, and familiar carols streamed from the stereo as I gazed at the crooked, balding tree. Still, something was missing. Meanwhile Greg and his parents arranged our unopened gifts in several neat piles.

By the time we were ready to open the presents, I was on the verge of falling asleep in one of the living room chairs.

"Look, Mommy," I heard Alex chirp. "Look, Mommy!"

Emerging from an exploratory expedition in the storage closet where we had been hiding the gifts, Alex cradled a golden treasure in his arms—my dime-store angel.

Stunned, I motioned him to bring the cherished memento to me. "That's an angel, Alex. Can you say 'angel'?"

"AIN-gel," he repeated.

"This angel belongs on the very top of the Christmas tree," I said. "Have Daddy lift you up so you can put it there."

The sight of Greg hoisting our son to plant the ragged angel on top of our equally well-worn tree made my eyes well with tears. When Alex returned to my arms and my round belly, I tousled his curls and embraced both of my little angels as I finally felt the warmth of the Christmas spirit.

Apparently the angel tree-topper—like the Christmas spirit itself—had been with me in Florida all along. All I needed to do was make the effort to find it.

Golumpki (Pigs in a Blanket)

—Robyn Kurth

1 CUP WHITE RICE

2 CUPS WATER

2 MEDIUM-SIZED CABBAGE HEADS

2 LARGE VIDALIA ONIONS

1 CUP (TWO STICKS) MARGARINE

1/4 TSP PEPPER, PLUS A PINCH FOR FINAL SEASONING

1/4 TSP SALT, PLUS A PINCH FOR FINAL SEASONING

1 TBSP ONION POWDER

4 CANS (10 3/4 OZ) CAMPBELL'S CONDENSED TOMATO SOUP

1 CAN (14 OZ) BEEF BROTH

1/2 TSP SUGAR

3 LBS GROUND SIRLOIN

2 EGGS

1. Preheat oven to 350 degrees F. Combine 1 cup of rice with 2 cups of water in a covered saucepan and heat until it just begins to boil. Turn off the heat, cover the saucepan, and let the rice continue cooking itself for about 5 minutes.

2. In the meantime, fill a large pot halfway full of water and boil the water. Add one head of cabbage and let it boil for about 4 minutes. As the cabbage leaves loosen, cut them individually from the base of the stalk and lay them out to cool in a large roaster pan equipped with a lid. Cut away the thick stem at the base of each leaf and discard. Repeat for second head of cabbage.

3. Chop the onions and sauté them in margarine in a large skillet. Add salt, pepper, and onion powder.

4. Combine tomato soup and beef broth in another pot. Add sugar to the mixture (up to a 1/2 cup of water can be added if the sauce appears to be too thick). Simmer on low heat while you assemble the *golumpki*.

5. Mix the ground sirloin with eggs. Add the sautéed onions and rice. Mix thoroughly. Use your hands to form a small round patty and place it on top of a cabbage leaf. Wrap the sides of the leaf over the beef patty and roll it up until it is completely covered. Put a little of the sauce on the bottom of the pan, and then place the cabbage roll into the roaster pan. Repeat until all of the beef mixture has been wrapped up in the cabbage leaves. Chop any remaining leaves and sprinkle over the *golumpki*.

6. Pour the tomato soup mixture over the *golumpki*. Lightly sprinkle with salt and pepper. Make sure the sauce does not go more than halfway up the sides of the roaster pan; the extra sauce will be used for serving.

7. Cover the roaster pan and cook at 350 degrees F for the first hour. Reduce the heat to 325 degrees F for another 1 to 1 1/2 hours.

Meatball Madness

By Candace Simar

In my family of origin, food is our love language. Especially at Christmas.

We may not speak of the strong affection we feel for each other, but we eat—eat and keep eating when we are together. Ruby's pickled beets, Inga's brownies, and Auntie Nora's buns fill the Christmas table end to end. It's what we do. And we do it well.

Annie took this feeding frenzy to new heights years ago when she hosted Christmas Tea. Using only the prettiest and most formal dishes, she served elegant desserts, finger-length sandwiches, truffles in crystal punch bowls, and Sally's macaroni salad with real crab. Only the women of the family were invited, the aunts and nieces, with everything formal and lovely, while harp music played in the background and Annie's Martha Stewart–like Christmas tree lit up the living room like a glowing star.

The men ogled the bulging table with disbelief before they shuffled downstairs to the family room, grumbling all the way. "Why weren't we invited? We like sandwiches. We like truffles. We like seven varieties of olives."

When the women finished their holiday extravaganza, the men and boys swooped in like hungry seagulls, pecking away at the leftovers, squawking about the inequity of it all, complaining about the small portions.

The next Christmas, we sisters each contributed something to ease Annie's workload for this new family tradition—and invited the men and nephews. It was such a success that the following year we begged for another increase in the guest list. What about our second cousin from White Bear Lake? What about the Omaha in-laws? Couldn't my best friend, going through a messy divorce, join us? With each added guest, we sisters brought more food, despite Annie's insistence that we had more than enough.

Last year, Linda, the oldest, almost ruined Christmas Tea by bringing enough Swedish meatballs to feed the state of Minnesota.

"That's it!" Annie's eyes blazed as she shoved yet another ice cream bucket of meatballs into her refrigerator. "You can't bring this much food! I can't take it anymore!" We stared at her in horror. "You can't really expect all of us to eat this much. We can't do it," she said as tears dripped down her face and splashed on her gravy-spattered arms. "Unless you promise to bring less food next year, the tea is canceled!"

Solemnly, we vowed to bring only what we were assigned. Nothing more. Not even if we were tempted. Not even if we found something on sale or stumbled across a great recipe.

"And no meatballs next year!" Annie insisted. "Never another meatball at Christmas Tea or I'll lock the doors on you."

This year, in charge of salads, I brought only one giant lettuce salad and limited myself to a single bottle of gourmet dressing.

Craisins added a touch of color on top of sliced hard-boiled eggs. The leafy greens looked great in my best crystal bowl.

"I hope you didn't bring too much." Annie met me at the door. "This year will be different."

And so it seemed. Manageable amounts of salad. Fewer buns. Enough pickled beets to send home with the second cousin from White Bear Lake. Not too many. Just enough. We did it. We cut back.

But as I washed my hands to help fix the sandwiches, I saw Annie's egg salad and mentioned it was larger than we needed. "I only used two dozen eggs," she said, defending herself, "because I didn't want to run short."

"The recipe calls for four eggs," I pointed out, "enough for sixteen finger sandwiches. What you made would feed an army!"

After a moment of hedging, Annie pulled a giant mixing bowl filled with ham salad out of the refrigerator. Enough to feed the entire state of Minnesota. Much more ham salad per capita than the meatballs of the year before.

"What were you thinking?" I stared in disbelief. "We can't possibly use this much ham salad."

"Without meatballs," she said in a quiet voice, "I was afraid we'd run out of food." She bit her lip and looked away. "And, anyway, the ham was a freebie from the grocery store." Were those tears in her eyes? "It only weighed twelve pounds . . . and Jordan had so much fun turning Mom's grinder."

This family needed help. I wondered aloud if there was a support group for perpetual food pushers of Norwegian descent. If not, we might start one . . . the sooner the better.

The next day I phoned to thank Annie for the lovely party. "I got rid of all the ham salad," she said with pride. "Every last bit. Sent it home with Claudia. Made Dede and Tommy take a bowl. Sent a ziplock along to Omaha. Made sandwiches for Nathan's lunch tomorrow."

"Nathan's a vegetarian," I said. "He just took the sandwiches to be nice."

"At least it's gone," she said with a happy sigh of relief. "It was a great Christmas Tea."

And that's the other thing about my family of origin. We like to make other people eat like we do. It's how we show our affection. It's how we expect them show it back to us. It's how we do things. And how I'm sure we'll do it next Christmas, too.

The Proof Is in the Pudding

By Donna Rushneck

Many families have a special custom that puts the joy and magic in Christmas. For us, it is Mom's chocolate bread pudding, as traditional as the wreath on the front door.

My older brother Bill liked the pudding soaked in milk with a sprinkle of sugar. My younger brother Jerry and I mounded it with whipped cream.

"You kids are ruining a good thing with all that stuff," Dad always said. "It's perfect right out of the pan."

We took for granted that Mom and her chocolate bread pudding would always be part of Christmas. But we unexpectedly lost Mom to cardiac arrest one October. Gloom hung over the family and drained all joy out of the upcoming holidays.

As the only daughter, I opted to host Christmas dinner and wanted to surprise the family by serving pudding. On a Saturday morning in early December, I decided to give the recipe a trial run. I got out Mom's oldest cookbook and, on a tattered page marked by an old Christmas card, I found a recipe—for plain bread pudding. To my consternation, there was no alternative listed for chocolate. I scanned Mom's other cookbooks, as well as my own, but none of them offered a chocolate bread pudding recipe.

A lump crowded my throat. Then I thought to call Aunt Cora. But she didn't know how Mom made the family favorite, either.

"I remember that your dad once said he loved bread pudding and wished it could be chocolate," Aunt Cora said. "Maybe your Mom just experimented until she got it right."

If Mom found a way, I thought, *so can I.*

As I prepared the recipe from the tattered page, I vaguely recalled "helping" Mom make bread pudding when I was a young child. I remembered her adding cocoa to the sugar, so I stirred together equal amounts and added them to the rest of the ingredients. Although there were lumps of cocoa in the batter, I figured they would dissolve during the baking process.

When I lifted the pudding from the oven, it looked strange. Spotted. I spooned a bite, blew on it, and nibbled. The chocolate lumps tasted bitter.

I felt my eyes sting with disappointment, and I slumped in defeat at the kitchen table.

"Why are you sad, Mommy?" Eight-year-old Shelley snuggled against me.

"I tried to make Grandma's Christmas pudding but it didn't turn out right."

Shelley stared into the pan. "That doesn't look like Grandma's pudding."

"It doesn't taste like it either." I forced a smile through my sigh.

"I helped Grandma make the pudding last year." She reached for the open cookbook still on the table. "I remember how."

She pointed at the recipe. "Mommy, you put the sugar in a bowl and add the rest of the stuff." Shelley smiled ear to ear. "And I'll do the important thing that Grandma said makes the pudding special."

My first inclination was not to repeat the fiasco. But Shelley was so eager and confident that I decided to chance it.

While I poured sugar into the mixing bowl, Shelley read the handles of the measuring cups. "Grandma said to use the cup with the one and a three on it."

She spooned cocoa into the one-third cup then dumped it into the bowl of sugar. Using the back of a spoon, Shelley pressed the mixture against the bowl. *Just like Mom once taught me*, I suddenly realized, my childhood memory sharpening.

Shelley squeezed the brown beads of cocoa between her fingertips. "Grandma said it's really important to get out all the lumps."

As I watched my daughter's little fingers working the batter, I could hear my mother's directions to me when I was a child helping her bake: *"Now, Donna, this is an important job. Mix the sugar and cocoa really good."*

For a few moments, I was a little girl again back in Mom's kitchen and I could feel her patient presence.

A few weeks later, I produced a perfect chocolate bread pudding for our first somber holiday without Mom. Every face brightened when I brought it to the Christmas table.

"I didn't think we'd ever have this again." Dad cleared his throat. "Now it feels more like Christmas."

I put my arm around my daughter. "If it weren't for Shelley, we wouldn't have the pudding." My eyes pooled and my voice cracked. "She remembered the part that makes it special."

More importantly, so had I. I'd been reminded that Mom's love would always be with us—just like her recipe for chocolate bread pudding.

Mom's Chocolate Bread Pudding

—Donna Rushneck

Yield: 6 servings

8 SLICES OF ITALIAN BREAD, WITH CRUSTS

1/3 CUP COCOA

1/2 CUP SUGAR

3 LARGE EGGS

1/4 TSP SALT

4 CUPS MILK

1/4 CUP BUTTER OR MARGARINE

1. Preheat oven to 300 degrees F.

2. Grease a 9-x-13 baking dish.

3. Tear bread into chunks and place in baking dish. Add cocoa to sugar and blend thoroughly until all cocoa lumps are gone.

4. In large bowl, add cocoa/sugar mixture to eggs and beat until creamy. Incorporate salt and milk.

5. Pour mixture over bread and dot with butter. Let stand 15 minutes.

6. Bake covered for 30 minutes. Remove cover and bake an additional 30 minutes. Remove from oven when a knife inserted in the center comes out clean. (A little additional baking time may be required.)

The Pied Pepper

By Jaye Lewis

epper was a brown and white, floppy-eared bundle of warm puppy breath. He was given to me on my tenth birthday, and from the moment he was placed in my arms we became the best of friends. We were inseparable.

Pepper was smart, too, a regular circus dog. He learned each trick in a single lesson. Except one: Pepper couldn't learn to sit up and beg. I held him up. I supported his back. But Pepper always went limp and slid to the floor. Of course, I hated for anyone to see that side of Pepper. Instead, I showed off his other tricks.

When someone asked if he could beg, I answered, "He would if there was something worth begging for."

On Christmas Eve, Pepper settled himself near the heavenly smells drifting from the oven. When my mother lifted out our family favorite, a deep-dish pumpkin pie, Pepper did it—he sat up straight, curled his little paws, and *begged!*

He sat, candy cane stiff, for a long, long moment.

"Why, look at you!" Mom's throaty laugh was as warm as the pumpkin pie she placed on top of the stove. She covered all the holiday pies with a long sheet of waxed paper and glanced at the clock. "Get your things together. It's time for church."

After the midnight Christmas Eve service, we invited friends home for coffee and pie. We drove to our mobile home and tumbled out of our cars, shushing one another in the darkness of the late hour and trying not to laugh.

The first thing Mom did was brighten the small room by plugging in the festive tree lights. In spite of the excitement of company, Pepper didn't bother to greet us. He didn't budge from his cozy spot on the couch near the oven.

I sat next to Pepper, but he didn't even look up.

All of a sudden, my mother gasped. "Oh my goodness!"

Mom was choking. No, she was crying. No—she was laughing. *Laughing?*

"Come look at this, everyone." Mom shifted the wax paper from the pies. Sitting in the middle of four untouched fruit pies was the deep-dish pumpkin—with a carefully eaten-out center. On either side of the cavernous hole were two little paw prints.

I knew Pepper was in for it. He had spoiled the sacred pie. Now he was going to die for his dastardly deed, and it was my mother who was going to kill him.

"Pepper," Mom commanded, "come here."

Pepper's head popped up. He knew that voice. Everybody knew that voice. Even if you didn't have a tail, you found one just so you could tuck it between your legs when you heard that voice.

Pepper slithered reluctantly off the couch and slinked to my mother. With his head hanging, he cowered at her feet.

She bent low and held the Christmas pie in front of him. "What did you do?" Her face was stern. "Did you eat this pie?"

The rest of us eyed each other, held our breaths, and waited for The Lecture.

"Pepper!" Mom peered into the small dog's face and ordered, "Beg!"

Pepper jerked to attention. He sat up, back ruler-straight and front paws perfectly curled.

"Here, Pepper." Mom's face softened as she placed the prized pumpkin pie on the floor. "Merry Christmas. You earned it."

Pepper had finally found something worth begging for!

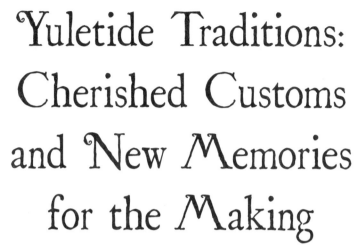

Yuletide Traditions:
Cherished Customs
and New Memories
for the Making

Log Cabin Christmas

By John Winsor

Sometime after midnight, the snowstorm stopped and bright stars pinpointed a carbon void. The fleeing storm cloud still cloaked the moon; there were no beams dancing across our floor. I tucked the goose-down quilt under my chin and scooched over to the warmth of Tish's body and smiled with anticipation of a day filled with family and Christmas tradition.

We woke to the smells of brewing coffee, sizzling bacon, and pine logs burning in the fireplace, to the sounds of footsteps and muted conversations and laughter. Our three kids, their spouses, and our eight grandkids were here, all fourteen, for the annual celebration at our cabin nestled along a freestone river in northwestern Wyoming. To relieve Tish of the chores, they'd formed interfamily teams to cook, set the table, and wash the dishes.

The rising sun brushed the top of snow-covered Pilot Peak, creating an alpenglow, a reddish tinge that plunged down the mountain as the sun climbed. The entire world snapped into vivid colors, a vast cerulean sky, miles of untracked snow, emerald green pines, and darker-tinged spruce, all framed by white mountains slashed by dark granite outcroppings. A fine Christmas Eve day.

Someone rang the old locomotive bell perched atop a log pole near the front door—five minutes until breakfast. We joined family on the couch, warmed by the fire, drank hot chocolate and coffee, and made plans for the day: Get the kids dressed for a crystalline ten-below morning, snap on cross-country skis, track to the forest through unbroken snow, spend an eternity selecting the perfect Christmas tree, cut it, sled it back, put it up, and, after all that effort, chow down again.

I watched each of the grandchildren—aged five to twenty— take turns with the ax (some with guidance from their fathers) to fell the tree. After lunch, the grandkids took great joy in decorating it, particularly when they found the holiday ornaments containing photographs they'd given Tish and me when they were young.

I watched and remembered my own excitement when I was their age, and later, a different kind of excitement when helping our children, John, Susan, and Tom. I realized this tradition of joy and anticipation now spanned three generations. Feeling the passage of time, I backed off to let them take the lead with their own children.

After the tree was decorated, naps taken, grace said, dinner served, and dishes washed, we gathered near the fireplace and watched flames crackle around the logs.

Someone distributed sheets of Christmas carols and began to lead us in song. Several grandchildren rolled their eyes and slunk away but, after hearing a chorus of "Jingle Bells," the slinkers returned and took up voice.

After we'd sung out, we read aloud Christmas stories about

Mary and Joseph and Bethlehem and the three wise men and Baby Jesus.

Finally, Susan urged the children to bed "because you-know-who might be coming tonight." Older kids cast knowing glances, while the believers hustled about the kitchen, selecting cookies, pouring milk, and placing plate and glass on the half-log bench in front of the fire.

Someone suggested they should leave a note for Santa, and everyone wanted to write their own. The little ones grabbed a piece of paper and a crayon, flopped on their bellies in front of the fire, and drew passable words and symbols of love and hope.

All the little kids hustled to their cabins to say their prayers and go to bed. Finally, it was quiet in the main cabin.

After a while the older ones, nonbelievers, drifted back from the circle of cabins, and we pulled boxes from hiding places. They helped me don the outfit: black boots trimmed in white, red baggy pants, a pillow tied to an already ample waist, a red, white-trimmed coat, wide black belt, and white gloves. Fourteen-year-old granddaughters Becca and Caroline did their special work: rouged cheeks, colored lips, adjusted white wig just so, combed beard, and perched glasses on nose. Not too far down, not too high, but just right.

After final inspections, I was escorted—just like I had been each of the past nineteen years—to the back door, out of sight from the other cabins. Tom handed me a huge sack filled with brightly wrapped gifts, and John handed me the sleigh bells and said that he'd return to his cabin and turn the porch light off when all was ready.

The snow was calf-deep, soft, silent, and a full moon rose on the eastern horizon, casting tree shadows. Bright reflection from the snow turned the cabins into black silhouettes. Slipping through the trees behind the cabins, I circled until I was in position. I waited for the signal.

The porch light snapped off.

Sleigh bells tinkled, the ring slicing through crystalline air, echoing in the night.

Hunched over by the weight of a sackful of surprises, I waddled past the cabins, ignoring excited movement at windows.

"Ho, ho, ho! Merry Christmas!"

I heard a door open and spotted little fellas scrambling onto the porch, held in check by their mom and dad. "Hi Santa! Hi Santa!" they shouted and waved.

I acted surprised and laughter rolled from deep inside my belly. I waved back and toddled through moonlight and snow toward the main cabin. Later, after I stacked presents under the tree, I sat by the fire nibbling a cookie.

Daughter-in-law Bridget sneaked back into the room. "When I put the boys back to bed, little Harry said he would never get to sleep. So I asked, 'Why not?'"

"And what did Harry say?" I asked.

Eyes moist, she gave me a hug and whispered, "'Because I have Santa's laughter in my heart.'"

A fine Christmas Eve, indeed.

Tea for You

By Jean Richert as told to Carol McAdoo Rehme

The holidays were flying on swift wings this year, but I was ready. Right on schedule. Tree, gifts, stockings, cards, decorating. All done ahead so that I could fully enjoy today's traditional celebration.

With my two children conveniently situated at the sitter's house, I took a minute to think. "Let's see," I scanned the dining room, "have I forgotten anything?"

I straightened the holly-leafed tea set; it was, after all, about the Christmas tea. My Windsong china ringed the walnut table. The silver-plated flatware I inherited from my grandmother—and polished, spoon by spoon, fork by fork for this occasion—flanked the place settings. *Perfect.* My hand-blown crystal stood at attention to the right of each plate. And, beneath it all, lay a crisp linen tablecloth freshly ironed.

"The napkins!" I hurried to fold the matching cloth squares into the crisp points of a bishop's mitre and placed them around the table.

Scrumptious scents of minted tea, seasonal desserts, and tempting appetizers wafted from the kitchen. But, to my way of thinking, the food was secondary. It was the setting, the center-piece, the time-honored, minute details that would delight my seasoned guests. They were, after all, the sole reason I was willing to "put on the dog" as my friend Marie would say.

And in they came, lonely elders and widows and friends, all of a different vintage who, themselves, once entertained with a flair for formality and an eye towards decorum. Who once welcomed Christmas with unlined faces and the boundless energy of youth.

I knew that's what drew them to my annual holiday tea. I made certain every detail harkened back to yesteryear and spoke to a more genteel era in their lives, when there was more leisure time to linger over a fragrant cup. And that was exactly why I delighted in providing the experience each year—the Girlfriend Christmas Tea that crossed the generations.

"Happy holidays!" I greeted the first guest. "May I take your coat?"

"Merry Christmas, Marilyn. Let me hold your gloves and hand-bag while you unbutton your jacket."

"Why, Wanda, what a lovely holiday brooch."

Marie, the eldest of the group at ninety-three, needed my close attention with her cane and over boots.

And so the gracious lunch proceeded.

Dressed to the nines in their best pumps and nicest jewelry, the ladies dined with classic deportment—interspersed with lively discussions, reminiscences of Christmases past, even poetic recitations mined from memories of school days long ago.

I paused in my own conversation and glanced around the table to rejoice in the moment. Be-ringed hands fluttered over heirloom silver. Behind rimmed glasses, faded eyes sparkled enough to rival the shine of my crystal. The scent of lilac talcum powder and Taboo perfume drifted across the table to co-mingle comfortably with peppermint tea.

And, beneath it all, reedy voices rose and flowed, caught up in the heady mixture of company, Christmas, and auld lang syne.

I smiled in satisfaction. *Next year*, I thought, *I believe I'll invite a few others*. My mind raced ahead with anticipation. *I'll simply put an extra leaf in the table, arrange transportation for my additional guests . . . and brew another pot of Christmas tea.*

Holiday Blockbuster

By Debbi Wise

Throughout the holidays, my mind performs flashbacks from my childhood in Memphis, Tennessee, with memorable images that rerun like the *Charlie Brown Christmas* special featured year after year on TV.

When it came to Christmas, my mother was a leading contender in the category of Best Production. Funding was tight, making it a low-budget show, but for the audience—the four Walker kids—it was always a blockbuster hit!

The season officially opened after the last Thanksgiving plate was washed and the pumpkin pie was served. Dad would bring out the box of tangled Christmas lights, furrow his brow, and make his annual declaration: "Guess I should test these to see if they still work."

Before long, all the brown tattered boxes were down from the attic. Rummaging through the decorations felt like a fond visit with relatives who made an appearance only once a year. As the excitement accelerated, my parents would decide it was time to buy a tree. Before long we were driving home with an evergreen tied to the top of our Chevy.

I was always convinced we had the best pick of the selection sold from Al's Christmas Trees, regardless if Dad had to surgically reshape the trunk and curse under his breath to get it into the stand. He hauled it inside, leaving a trail of pine needles on the shag carpeting. Clogging the vacuum with the prickly spikes was as much a tradition as placing the star on top of the tree. The scent of fresh pine was ripe in our home as we hung ornaments while sipping hot chocolate sprinkled with bobbing miniature marshmallows.

Christmas was the only time we received gifts. In our family of six, money was stretched thin all year. My parents conserved the best they could, making sure our basic needs were met, but there was nothing to spare for luxuries. So at Christmas, I felt like Dorothy when she stepped out of black-and-white and into the colorful Land of Oz. Knowing I was standing in Christmas was almost enough for me!

As wrapped gifts were placed beneath the tree, my sister and I shook only the packages tagged with our names. Though our gifts were meager, they put a spark in our eyes. We were always pleased.

When I was three years old, my sister and I received doll beds crafted by Dad. The next year we got a tea set arranged on a small wooden table with little chairs, more evidence of his ingenuity. It never crossed my mind that these gifts should come from a store. After all, they were handmade especially for us.

Since our mother knew her way around a Singer sewing machine, each year she used her skill to earn extra Christmas money. The Barbie doll outfits she designed and sold easily competed with those sold at local stores and padded the Christmas fund so well one year that my sister and I were the recipients of bicycles—our first. Never mind that they were used. When it's magic, you don't see anything but matching blue bikes. And Mom made sure Christmas was magic for me—for all of us.

My mother's script for Christmas was handed down to me like her recipe for holiday turkey. The magic, I learned, was all about the *waiting*. Holding out, not overindulging during the year. That was her key ingredient. It was an easy habit to practice, since, like my mother, I had to work within a tight budget.

I stuck to the script closely; only once do I recall a misstep. Two days before Christmas we took our three-year-old daughter to see Santa at the mall. She was well prepped with the items I convinced her she wanted: a miniature sink and stove, a Little Mermaid play tent, and the homemade doll bed I received when I was her age.

From her perch on Santa's lap, Hailey shyly recited her list and added, "And Santa, I want a red fire engine."

Huh? I thought. *A fire engine? Where did that come from?*

On the way home, I asked about her odd request.

"That's my special surprise I wanted to ask Santa for," Hailey chirped.

I chewed on a broken nail, mulling over what I would do. My budget was depleted and it was two days before Christmas. There was no way I would have time to fight the last-minute shoppers. Banking on the fact that she was as forgetful as a new puppy, I went about the business of preparing the best Christmas possible.

On Christmas morning, the house was full of relatives taking photos of my two sleepy-eyed daughters as they scampered downstairs to see what Santa delivered. Hailey stood in front of her gifts, her puffy baby cheeks smiling. She looked around, exclaiming over everything, and then said something I had hoped not to hear. "Santa forgot my fire truck."

One of her aunts quickly diverted Hailey's attention to the doll bed. I sighed in relief when, distracted by her new Little Mermaid tent, my daughter climbed inside to play.

After a few minutes of excited chattering and giggling, however, Hailey emerged with a grin on her face—and a little red fire engine in her hand.

"That Santa tricked me," she said. "He hid my fire truck in the tent!"

For a moment, everyone was speechless. To this day, no one has ever admitted to the deed.

When my girls grew up, I knew it was time to bequeath the family Christmas script. I never questioned its origins, assuming it was inherited like DNA, the way brown eyes or big ears get passed on from one generation to the next. And I would have gone on believing that. But a letter arrived from Mom.

She touched on a few delicate issues in the letter and then talked about her lonely childhood. My eyes blurred as I read the words she had written: "I never had a Christmas with decorations, packages, or the experience of a tree."

How a person never exposed to the love and excitement of a traditional holiday could pull off such a perfect performance was beyond me. In my eyes, it was like walking onto a Broadway stage and knowing the lines without ever reading the script. Yet, for my mother, there was no inheritance—she simply made it up.

Or did she?

When I look to a loving God, and the true meaning behind Christmas, I see his image in my mother. His was the script she followed. His was the same script she handed down for me to share with my children. I am passing his script to my children to share with their children. And that's the Best Production of all.

What a Card

By Andrea Langworthy

When people tell me they have cut their holiday card list in half, I cringe. Even with the increase in postage and the high price of greeting cards, I can't think of one person I would eliminate. In fact, my roster grows every Christmas.

I send cards to people we haven't seen in twelve years and neighbors we wave to every morning as they drive off to work. I include friends who sent a card last year and those who have never sent one. Inside each card I write a message: "Happy Holidays" or "Let's get together soon."

My husband learned early that as much as I like sending cards this time of year, I love being on the receiving end even more. When he returns home each night after a long day at work, do I greet him at the door with a hug and a kiss of gratitude? No, I grab the mail from his hands and rush to the living room to see who has sent us their very best.

Even as a child, I couldn't wait until the postal carrier dropped a load of cards through the slot next to our front door. Those were the years everyone sent tidings, necessitating two mail deliveries on the days closest to Christmas. Ah, the good old days . . .

Long before the advent of word-processed form letters or fancy paper imprinted with candy canes and poinsettias, my mother's friend wrote an annual letter (typing each one individually on plain, white paper) that was a highlight of my Christmas season. I awaited its arrival, eager to read the latest news about this woman's children who, though close to my age, were so different from me. First, they lived in California, home to Hollywood and Disneyland. Second, these children were perfect. The letter said so, year after year.

I wanted to meet the daughter, so beautiful her father had to "beat packs of potential boyfriends away from the back door." I hoped for a glimpse of the son, a golden-haired Charles Atlas, certain to become a professional athlete or a movie star, so smart he could be the president, too.

"Just once," I heard my father say, "I'd like to hear the truth about those little brats."

I looked at Mom to see if Dad could be right, but all she said was, "Shush, Arthur."

Over the years, I've thought about penning my own Christmas letter. After all, I call myself a writer. But the dilemma remains: truth or fiction? I relish every word of the letters I receive and appreciate the effort of the sender, but who would want to hear that we went way over budget when we redecorated? Certainly, I would need to embellish the story of last year's winter vacation when we went nowhere and did nothing.

I'm afraid my holiday letter might receive the same reaction my daughter gave to one in my card basket this year. Folding the epistle in crisp fourths, she said in measured tones, "This is why I do not write Christmas letters."

She's right.

And so, I will continue to send my seasonal greetings. But my message this year will be brief and to the point: Happy Holidays. We should get together soon.

 For ideas and creative inspiration for your holiday newsletter, see page 223.

Cumbered Christmas

By Wanda Quist

The New Testament says Martha was "cumbered about much serving" and wanted Jesus to bid her sister Mary to help her. But Jesus said, "Martha, thou art careful and troubled about many things: but one thing is needful: and Mary hath chosen that good part . . ."

At Christmastime, I was Martha in the Bible. Every year.

I was "cumbered about much serving" with my daily duties as a mother of eight children. Every holiday, Martha-like, I became "troubled about many things," as the expectations of a traditional celebration came around again. In short, I was overwhelmed.

I chipped away at the gift list. "What should we buy your parents?" I asked Robert early in the month, when there was still time to mail their package to Canada. "And what new Colorado mementoes can we send to my family in Oregon?"

I labored over the holiday newsletter. It was no small matter to condense a year's worth of activities and adventures into two pages (or less), and be entertaining.

I tackled the kitchen. I climbed onto a stepladder and retrieved the blue glass cookie jar while the kids called out their favorites.

"Toffee squares!"

"Peanut butter blossoms!"

"Chocolate chip!

"Sandies!"

We needed lots of cookies to last through the month of December. We filled plates for neighbors, friends, and teachers. We baked until we had no more room to stash cookies. Only then did I start making the fruitcakes.

I directed the seasonal decorating.

"We're always the last people to put up our tree," the kids whined.

In preparation, we moved furniture and vacuumed—everything. The kids helped assemble and decorate the artificial tree. To make certain each had a fair share, I counted red balls, blue balls, and painted wooden ornaments and doled them out. I placed each of the special keepsakes on the tree myself.

I orchestrated all the Christmas programming.

With our large family, holiday concerts meant trips to elementary, middle, and high schools. I always scheduled one family evening to look at lights, sing carols, and deliver those plates of cookies. I calendared my husband's office party as well as the church social. When events conflicted, Robert went to one while I attended the other. *Divide and conquer.* That was my motto.

And, of course, I helped everyone buy or make one-of-a-kind gifts for each other.

Suffice it to say, the process involved lots of secret shopping excursions, tons of gift wrap, and hours of time, thought, and effort. December, everyone knew, was not the month to get sick or injured. There simply wasn't time.

All too soon, Christmas morning arrived with excited children sprawled around the still dark room, lit only by the tree lights.

Funny, but I can't remember any of those unique presents we labored so diligently over. Robert and I don't go caroling now and there are no school programs to attend. I don't bake cookies and fruitcake, and I don't miss doing it. There are fewer packages to ship, and cleaning the house isn't as involved as it once was.

But one image is crystal clear.

Each of those Christmas mornings, we took time to gather for family prayer. We settled around the tree and read from the New Testament about the birth of our savior, Jesus Christ.

During those still, holy minutes, I gazed into each shining, upturned face and remembered why we celebrated Christmas. I remembered the "good part" that Mary knew.

Oh, there were ways I could have simplified, traditions I might have eliminated to feel less "cumbered." Honestly, I wish I had.

But I'm eternally grateful for the sweet, spiritual moments we shared as a family on those sacred mornings.

Mary Christmas.

The Best Time of the Year

Christopher Garry

Our family comes together
each year at Christmastime
with smiles, hugs, and presents
and Christmas bells that chime.

We sit around the fireplace,
sharing stories of our life . . .
the good times and the sad times,
the successes and the strife.

Smells come from the kitchen,
foretelling our holiday feast,
turkey and carrots and potatoes
and, of course, the roasted "beast."

Then around the great big table
all of us do squeeze.
We thank God for all we're given . . .
then, "Pass the gravy, please."

Yes, Christmastime is the time
when all the family's here.
That's why we all know
it's the best time of the year.

Must-Know Info
for Making
Things Merry

Must-Know Info

Channel Your Inner Martha: Host an Open House with Fabulous Food

Ivy Larson, healthy lifestyle expert, recipe developer, and coauthor of The Gold Coast Cure, *www.thegoldcoastcure.com*

Christmas—and the weeks surrounding the holiday—is a wonderful time to plan and host a festive open house. To take pressure off of yourself, you should serve an enticing variety of delicious dishes on buffet tables. This relaxed setup will allow your guests to eat at their own pace (and come back for seconds and thirds). Furthermore, an open house is a laid-back, yet fun way to celebrate the holiday season. Your guests can arrive at different times throughout the party, which will also help you to alleviate party "congestion" while enhancing the ambiance of the celebration.

I've selected an array of easy recipes that you can serve at room temperature, which will ensure that the get-together is considerably more enjoyable for you, the hostess. I am a firm believer that you should always have a good time at your own party! For an open house, it's also a good idea to offer a balance between bite-sized appetizers and heartier buffet-style fare. For this menu, the leg of lamb, Brussels sprouts hash, tabbouleh, and mixed greens salad can be displayed on a buffet, and the smaller appetizers like the crostini and the shrimp, can either be tray-passed or arranged on smaller tables.

Just because it is the holiday season, there is no excuse to derail your healthy eating habits. While this party food is intriguing and very flavor-forward, it's also super healthy. My ultimate open house dishes not only taste terrific, but you and your guests can enjoy them all without feeling guilty. All of the all-natural whole-foods recipes are considerably lower in saturated fat and much richer in good-for-you ingredients like fiber, omega-3 fats, and antioxidants, which are usually not found in standard holiday recipes. Additionally, none of my recipes contain trans fat, high fructose corn syrup, or refined carbohydrates (except for the modest amount of sugar in the dessert). Don't worry though—even the dessert has a healthy twist, as it is made with much less sugar than most sweet treats. Best of all, none of your guests will be complaining come New Year's Day, when they can still fit into their preholiday jeans!

WINTER OPEN HOUSE

MENU

Mint-Infused Leg of Lamb

Ivy Larson, recipe developer and coauthor,
The Gold Coast Cure, www.thegoldcoastcure.com

Unroll the roast and trim all visible fat using kitchen shears and a knife. Season both sides of the roast with salt and pepper.

In a blender, process together the mint leaves, lemon juice, olive oil, mint jelly, garlic, and applesauce.

Pour three-fourths of the marinade over the roast, reserving the rest for later. Cover and marinate the roast for at least six hours or overnight in the refrigerator.

Remove the roast from the marinade. Reroll the roast and secure it with twine at one-inch intervals.

Preheat the oven to 425 degrees F.

Bake for 50 minutes or until a meat thermometer registers 145 degrees F (medium rare) or degree of preference for doneness. Lamb is usually best when pink inside and crusty outside. Let the roast stand for 20 minutes before serving.

Bring the reserved marinade to a boil for two minutes. Pour over the lamb just before serving.

1 FOUR-POUND ROLLED BONELESS LEG OF LAMB, TRIMMED OF FAT

SALT AND FRESHLY GROUND PEPPER

1 CUP FRESH MINT LEAVES

JUICE FROM 2 WHOLE LEMONS

1/4 CUP EXTRA-VIRGIN OLIVE OIL

1/2 CUP MINT JELLY

3 GARLIC CLOVES, CHOPPED

1/4 CUP UNSWEETENED APPLESAUCE

Servings: 8

Gingered Brussels Sprouts Hash with Golden Raisins

Ivy Larson, recipe developer and coauthor,
The Gold Coast Cure, www.thegoldcoastcure.com

Heat 2 tablespoons of the extra virgin olive oil in a medium skillet over medium-high heat; add the ginger and shallots, season with salt and pepper to taste, and cook for about 8 minutes (or until shallots are softened). Add the vinegar and raisins and cook for an additional 3–4 minutes. Set shallots aside.

Heat the butter and remaining tablespoon of extra virgin olive oil in a large skillet over medium-high heat; add Brussels sprouts, season with salt and pepper to taste, and sauté for 6–7 minutes. Add the water and orange juice concentrate and cook for 8–10 minutes (or until the liquid evaporates).

Add the reserved shallots and season with salt and pepper to taste. Remove skillet from heat. Serve warm or at room temperature.

3 TABLESPOONS EXTRA VIRGIN OLIVE OIL, DIVIDED

1 TABLESPOON GRATED GINGER

2 LARGE SHALLOTS, THINLY SLICED

SALT, TO TASTE

FRESHLY GROUND BLACK PEPPER, TO TASTE

2 TABLESPOONS APPLE CIDER VINEGAR

1/4 CUP GOLDEN RAISINS

1 1/4 POUNDS BRUSSELS SPROUTS, TRIMMED, HALVED LENGTHWISE, AND CUT INTO 1/8-INCH SLICES

1 TEASPOON ORGANIC BUTTER

3/4 CUP WATER

1 TABLESPOON ORANGE JUICE CONCENTRATE

Servings: 4

Spicy Blackened Shrimp with Cranberry-Orange Salsa

Ivy Larson, recipe developer and coauthor,
The Gold Coast Cure, www.thegoldcoastcure.com

To make the salsa, combine the cranberries, cilantro, scallions, jalapeno pepper, and marmalade in a mini Cuisinart. Chop to medium consistency. Transfer mixture to a serving dish. Add orange segments and salt to taste. Refrigerate until serving time.

SALSA:

1 CUP FROZEN CRANBERRIES, THAWED

1/4 CUP CILANTRO, CHOPPED

1/3 CUP CHOPPED SCALLIONS

1 TABLESPOON JALAPENO PEPPER, SEEDED AND MINCED

3 TABLESPOONS ALL-NATURAL ORANGE MARMALADE

2 ORANGES, FINELY CHOPPED

SALT, TO TASTE

In a large zip-top bag, add paprika, cayenne pepper, garlic powder, ground cloves, cumin, oregano, and salt. Zip bag and shake to combine ingredients thoroughly.

Toss shrimp in 1 tablespoon extra virgin olive oil. Add shrimp to the bag with the spice mixture, zip the bag, and toss shrimp to coat. Remove shrimp from bag.

Heat one tablespoon of extra virgin olive oil in a large, nonstick skillet over medium-high heat. Add half of the seasoned shrimp and cook for about 2 minutes each side, or until done. Remove shrimp from pan. Repeat the procedure with the remaining tablespoon of oil and remaining seasoned shrimp. Serve warm or at room temperature with salsa.

SHRIMP:

1 TABLESPOON PAPRIKA

1/4 TEASPOON CAYENNE PEPPER

1 TEASPOON GARLIC POWDER

1/8 TEASPOON GROUND CLOVES

2 TEASPOONS CUMIN

1 TEASPOON OREGANO

1/2 TEASPOON SALT, PLUS MORE TO TASTE

1 1/2 POUNDS LARGE SHRIMP (ABOUT 36 TOTAL), PEELED AND DEVEINED

3 TABLESPOONS EXTRA VIRGIN OLIVE OIL, DIVIDED

Servings: 8

Mixed Greens Salad

Ivy Larson, recipe developer and coauthor,
The Gold Coast Cure, www.thegoldcoastcure.com

In a medium bowl, whisk the vinegar, olive oil, honey, mustard, salt, and pepper.

In a large bowl, toss the salad greens, pear slices, pecans, and feta cheese together. Add the vinaigrette to taste.

Serve immediately.

Servings: 8

FOR THE VINAIGRETTE:

4 TABLESPOONS APPLE CIDER VINEGAR

I CUP OLIVE OIL

2 TABLESPOONS HONEY

4 TEASPOONS DIJON MUSTARD

I TEASPOON SALT

I TEASPOON BLACK PEPPER

FOR THE SALAD:

16 CUPS MIXED BAGGED SALAD GREENS

4 RIPE PEARS, SLICED INTO THIN, LENGTHWISE STRIPS

I CUP CHOPPED PECANS

8 OUNCES LIGHT FETA CHEESE, CRUMBLED

Goat Cheese and Pistachio Nut Crostini

Ivy Larson, recipe developer and coauthor,
The Gold Coast Cure, www.thegoldcoastcure.com

Preheat oven to 400 degrees F.

Using a mini Cuisinart, process pistachios into fine crumbs. Add the goat cheese, parsley, 3 tablespoons of extra virgin olive oil, raw honey, lemon juice, and Parmesan. Process ingredients until thoroughly blended. Season to taste with salt. Set mixture aside.

Arrange the sixteen bread triangles on a cookie sheet. Brush bread with the remaining 2 tablespoons of extra virgin olive oil. In the preheated oven, toast bread for 10 minutes. Remove from oven. Spread toast with the pistachio cheese mixture, return to oven, and bake for an additional 3 minutes. Remove from oven and serve warm or at room temperature.

1/2 CUP SALTED PISTACHIOS

4 OUNCES GOAT CHEESE

1/4 CUP CHOPPED PARSLEY

5 TABLESPOONS EXTRA VIRGIN OLIVE OIL, DIVIDED

1 TEASPOON RAW HONEY

1 TABLESPOON LEMON JUICE

3 TABLESPOONS GRATED PARMESAN

SALT, TO TASTE

8 PIECES SPROUTED WHOLE GRAIN BREAD (SUCH AS EZEKIEL 4:9 BRAND), CRUST REMOVED, BREAD SLICES CUT IN HALF DIAGONALLY

Servings: 8–10

Tabbouleh with Mint and Cranberries

Ivy Larson, recipe developer and coauthor,
The Gold Coast Cure, www.thegoldcoastcure.com

Bring 4 1/2 cups of water to a boil in a large saucepan. Add the bulgur and simmer for 10–12 minutes or until all of the water is absorbed.

Meanwhile, place the cranberries and the remaining 3/4 cup of water in a microwave-safe bowl and microwave on high for 2 minutes; drain the water and blot the cranberries with paper towels to remove excess moisture.

When the bulgur is done, transfer the cooked grains to a large serving bowl and stir in the cranberries, pecans, diced cucumber, mint, oil, and salt and pepper to taste. Serve immediately.

NOTE: You can make this recipe up to two days in advance and store it in an airtight container.

4 1/2 CUPS OF WATER, PLUS 3/4 CUP (RESERVED)

2 CUPS BULGUR WHEAT

1 1/4 CUPS DRIED CRANBERRIES

3/4 CUP FINELY CHOPPED PECANS

2 SMALL CUCUMBERS, SEEDS REMOVED AND DICED

1/2 CUP FRESH MINT, RINSED, PATTED DRY, AND CHOPPED

2 TEASPOONS OLIVE OIL

SALT AND PEPPER, TO TASTE

Servings: 8

Santa's Spicy Molasses Cookies

Ivy Larson, recipe developer and coauthor,
The Gold Coast Cure, www.thegoldcoastcure.com

Combine sugar blend and baking butter in a large bowl; beat with a mixer at medium speed until light and fluffy. Add the molasses and the egg; beat well.

In a separate bowl, combine flour, baking soda, cinnamon, cloves, ginger, and salt, stirring with a whisk. Add the flour mixture to the sugar mixture; beat at low speed just until blended. Cover and freeze dough for one hour.

Preheat oven to 375 degrees F.

Place water in a small bowl, and place brown sugar in another bowl. Shape chilled dough into two-inch balls, and then flatten slightly into the shape of a cookie. Dip one side of each unbaked cookie in water; dip wet side in sugar.

Place the cookies, sugar side up, one inch apart on baking sheets coated with cooking spray.

Bake for 12–15 minutes or until cookies begin to brown. Remove from the pan and cool on a wire rack. Allow to cool or refrigerate for 10 minutes before serving.

1/2 CUP SPLENDA BROWN SUGAR BLEND FOR BAKING

1/2 CUP LAND O'LAKES SOFT BAKING BUTTER WITH CANOLA OIL

1/2 CUP MOLASSES

1 EGG

2 1/2 CUPS WHOLE WHEAT PASTRY FLOUR

2 TEASPOONS BAKING SODA

1 TEASPOON GROUND CINNAMON

1/2 TEASPOON GROUND CLOVES

1/2 TEASPOON GROUND GINGER

1/2 TEASPOON SALT

1/2 CUP WATER

1/4 CUP BROWN SUGAR

Servings: 20 cookies

Christmas Cran-Apple Martini

Ivy Larson, recipe developer and coauthor,
The Gold Coast Cure, www.thegoldcoastcure.com

Setting aside garnish, pour ice and liquids into a cocktail shaker and shake gently. Pour into four chilled martini glasses. Put several fresh cranberries into each glass and place red or green thinly sliced apples onto rims of glasses for garnish.

CUP OF ICE

1 1/2 CUPS ALL-NATURAL CRAN-APPLE JUICE

2 OZ. ABSOLUT CITRON VODKA

1 OZ. GRAND MARNIER

SPLASH OF APPLE CIDER

SQUEEZE OF LEMON JUICE

1/4 CUP FRESH CRANBERRIES, FOR GARNISH

1 RED OR GREEN APPLE, THINLY SLICED, FOR GARNISH

Servings: 4

Must-Know Info
How to Find the Perfect Christmas Tree

Rick Dungey, public relations manager,
National Christmas Tree Association (NCTA)

How do you find the perfect Christmas tree? What's the best kind of Christmas tree for your home? What aroma is most appealing to you? There are simply no straightforward answers to these questions. They are akin to asking someone what's the best tasting beer in the world. Anyone can probably rattle off their answer, but if you ask nineteen people, you're likely to end up with twenty different answers.

Christmas trees are the same way: opinions vary greatly on what makes one tree better than another. One thing that has been consistent in my years of answering questions about Christmas trees is that people tend to have strong emotions about trees that are just like the ones they had when they were kids. So whether you are looking for a wave of nostalgia or you are looking for something new and different, here are some basic guidelines that can help you get the best tree for your own home.

Species

There are more than thirty-five different species of trees grown as Christmas trees in North America. Spruce, pine, fir, cypress, cedar—the choices can seem bewildering. Most species of trees are not durable enough to be baled and shipped long distances. This means that many of them can only be harvested from local farms. You should begin your search on the National Christmas Tree Association (NCTA) species description page at http://www. christmastree.org/types.cfm. This page will provide you with a detailed description of the sixteen most common species. Then, you can decide if you prefer a short needle or a long needle tree. Needles can also be sharp or blunt; they can be round or flat. Trees are in different shades and hues, ranging from deep green to light blue. Once you decide your preferences on all of these variables, you can narrow your choices down and begin your search.

Shape

You also must consider the shape and density of your tree. Christmas trees don't automatically look like they do without a lot of work by the grower. You may desire a scraggly, Charlie Brown–type of tree with a lot of space between the branches. The "openness" of the tree is dependent somewhat on genetics, but mostly it is a result of the shearing practices of the grower. If you are looking for an open tree, check with farms and lots in your area and ask them if they have a "less sheared" tree or one that would be "graded a cull." If you use these terms, the grower will understand what you are looking for.

The width of a tree is another important consideration. Take my house, for example. I live in a 150-plus-year-old renovated row house with ten-foot ceilings but very narrow rooms. I must have a "skinny" tree. The height-width ratio is measured by what's called the "taper." Generally, most trees are sheared so that they can grow to an 80 percent taper. This means that a ten-foot-tall tree will be eight feet wide at the bottom. If you have a more narrow space, ask the retail lot or the farm for trees with a 50 or 60 percent taper.

Aroma

There's simply no denying that the most appealing characteristic of a Christmas tree is the aroma it produces. In countless "man on the street" type of interviews, when someone is asked what's so important about the aroma of a tree, he or she will say "because it smells like Christmas." The aroma is very subjective for each person—you must decide which tree smells the strongest and smells the best to you. The best way to find out what type of tree smells the best to you is to, well, go sniff some trees.

Overall Appearance

When it comes to interior design, some species (due to their needle type, general shape, branch stiffness, typical color/hue, etc.) work better with certain decorating styles or themes. For example, a white pine is a very common species that is grown east of the Rocky Mountains. It has a long, soft needle and is typically very bright green, with limp branches and twigs—it is a very full, dense tree. This tree also has a more formal and elegant look to it. If you're looking for a tree for a dining room and want to decorate it with some white lights and subtle bits of color inserted into the branches, the white pine would make an excellent choice.

You should think ahead about where the tree will be displayed, how it will be decorated, and what kind of overall impression you want it to make. This can help make your decision on some of the criteria listed above. Also, the great thing about farm-grown Christmas trees is that because there are so many different species grown in so many different styles, you can try a different one each year until you find one that's perfect for your home.

General Tips

For many years, the NCTA has published general tips on going to a retail lot and to a choose-and-cut farm to get a Christmas tree. You can find these at http://www.christmastree.org/selection. cfm. It really helps to read these tips (and any others provided specifically by the farm or the lot operator, if they have them) ahead of time. Choosing your tree should be a fun family event, not a hassle. If you decide to go out to a farm to cut your own tree, you will need some special information. These tips, which are on our website, will help you prepare. The NCTA also publishes a very comprehensive guide on caring for a cut Christmas tree at http://www.christmastree.org/care.cfm. You will find it helpful to read our care tips in advance of going to get a tree. Remember to purchase a good tree stand that can hold an adequate amount of water.

Over the years I have heard many different myths, legends, and fallacies regarding the right way to display and care for a cut Christmas tree. Some people come up with the strangest things. Our care tips at the NCTA are written by scientists who have conducted many controlled studies on moisture retention on many different species. The NCTA also helps to make it easy to find a local tree recycling program. Because cut Christmas trees are plants, they are also 100 percent biodegradable, and they should be recycled and returned to the earth. An environmental organization called Earth 911 maintains and updates a searchable database of Christmas tree recycling programs throughout North America. This site is free and easy to use. You can do a zip code search from the NCTA website or call 1-800-CLEAN UP. You can also recycle your tree on your own by using the branches to protect your plants and bulbs during cold winter months. You can also put out a whole tree that can be used for shelter by birds, small mammals, and other wildlife. Farm-grown Christmas trees will always decompose and contribute nutrients back into the soil.

You may not want to get a real Christmas tree because you think that it's too much of a hassle and that you will have to constantly vacuum up needles. Don't you vacuum regularly anyway? Is vacuuming really a special consideration? Even if you spend a couple of hours putting up a tree and a couple of hours taking it down after Christmas, isn't it worth it? To get a special feeling each time you walk into your home and "smell Christmas," and remember how much fun it was to choose and decorate your tree with family and/or friends, is worth a couple of hours of your time, in my opinion.

Merry Christmas and happy tree hunting! (Additional information can always be found at the NCTA website at www.real christmastrees.org. You can also read a Christmas tree blog and post questions at http://realtreetalk.blogspot.com/.)

Must-Know Info

Ten Ways to Beat the Holiday Blues

Melissa Roske, New York-based life and personal coach,
www.wheelsinmotioncoaching.com

If you are feeling as if you're adrift in a sea of holiday stress and strain—whether it's financial (how to pay for all the holiday gifts); emotional (how to deal with difficult friends and family members); or practical (how to do it all, with limited time and energy)—it's as normal as your desire to return those hideous PJs from your well-meaning Aunt Millie.

It's also normal to feel down in the dumps, especially if your holiday plans aren't packed with holiday cheer. The good news is that you can have a stress-free Christmas if you're armed with the right tools, and are in the right frame of mind. Here are ten suggestions to help you adjust your attitude and enjoy your holidays (without stressing out over them).

1. Watch your pennies.

Your kids have been begging for the latest Nintendo Wii; your sister has been longing for a Prada tote; and your husband has been hinting around for a new set of golf clubs. The "gimme" factor has definitely taken hold, and the list of "I-gotta-have-its" goes on and on.

Sure, it feels good to spend your hard-earned cash on those you love. The problem is not with the purchasing, but with the credit card bills that will be appearing in your mailbox next month (and for many months to come). Unfortunately, after the feel-good factor fades to that darker, uglier fear of: "How the heck am I going to PAY for all of this?" the panic usually sets in.

The secret—which is really not secret at all—is to pace yourself financially, stay within your budget, and not spend beyond your means. Not being able to splurge on the latest or greatest can be tough, and disappointing your friends and family is the last thing that you want to do. But staying awake at night worrying about how you're going to finance your holiday spending spree is far worse.

The stress-free solution? While store-bought gifts are surely the easy way out, the allure of homemade presents never goes out of style. Also, the feel-good giving factor is priceless.

2. Step away from the buffet!

Eating and drinking at holiday get-togethers may seem as natural as snow in December. But remember that overindulging comes with a high price tag: weight gain.

To avoid gaining extra padding this holiday season (and we're not talking about the down comforter on your king-sized bed), avoid overindulgence like the plague. That doesn't mean that you have to abstain from all yummy holiday fare—just don't use the holidays as an excuse to go nuts! The key? Moderation, moderation, moderation.

Also, noshing on a small but satisfying pre-party snack—a container of fat-free yogurt, a 100-calorie packet of microwave popcorn or oatmeal, ten almonds, or a cheese stick or two—will keep you from attacking the dessert table.

3. Plan ahead.

If you, like most Americans, buy the majority of your holiday gifts at the last minute, you're not doing yourself any favors. Not only does this split-second shopping create a definitive stress overload—not to mention poor decision making—it ends up costing you more money than if you'd planned ahead and done your holiday shopping before Labor Day.

Since turning back the clock isn't an option (who really thinks of buying snowshoes in September?), that doesn't mean that you can't plan ahead for next year. As soon as your tinsel has been tossed and your lights have been put away, hit the post-holiday sales and squirrel away your bargains for upcoming events all year long—birthdays, anniversaries, bridal and baby showers, and holiday gifts.

During this holiday season, remember to spend some time shopping online. Although you may not score any serious bargains, the savings you'll get in the sanity department will be well worth the price.

4. Keep expectations realistic.

For many of us, the holidays can be an emotionally nerve-racking time, with too much emphasis placed on being jolly and jovial. Obviously, not everybody feels like dancing around the

Yule log during the holiday season, especially if there's been a sad event, a tragedy, or a loss in the family (a death, divorce, separation, etc).

If you can keep your eye on the prize—gratitude for health, a lovely home, a fulfilling job, a supportive family, and a great group of friends—you're less likely to feel blue because your life isn't a sunshine-filled bed of roses (which is overrated anyway).

5. Live in harmony (or at least fake it).

Holidays tend to bring families together—which is not always a good thing, especially if your family is more Osbourne than Osmond. Try to remember that no family is perfect, and yours doesn't have to be either.

At the same time, the holidays are not the time for over-wrought emotional confrontations, ugly family feuds, or airing of dirty linen. If you're mad at your Aunt Blanche for _____ (pick a transgression), there's no rule saying that you can't keep it to yourself. Your living room does not need to resemble a *Jerry Springer* soundstage. In other words, back off—it's Christmas.

The bottom line: avoid emotional family confrontations, at least until the mistletoe has been tossed in the trash.

6. Reach out and touch someone.

If you find yourself singing the blues instead of "Jingle Bells," why not turn your sorry solo into a more uplifting duet or trio? Not only will connecting with others help raise your spirits, sharing your time with others will add structure and purpose to your hectic routine.

Volunteerism, for instance, is an excellent way to share the

love. Perhaps you can lend a hand at a local soup kitchen or at a
homeless shelter. Or, if you have a special talent like playing the
piano or tap dancing, showcasing your skills at a local senior citizens' center or at a children's hospital might be perfect for you.
The point is, you have a lot to give, not just to yourself but to
others. What you'll get in return will be immeasurable.

7. Delegate tasks.

Sure, everyone thinks that you're a superhero, and in many
ways, you are. Despite the fact that you are constantly going
many places and doing many things, that doesn't mean that you
need to do all of the holiday shopping, wrap all of the gifts, clean
the entire house, cook, serve, and clean up all of the meals—and
stay in a cheery holiday mood all at the same time. You deserve
some help!

Asking is one way to get help, but telling those around you
what you expect—and need—from them is the most effective
way to get things done. "Don't ask, don't tell" doesn't work in the
military, and it won't work for you during the holiday season. So
ask and tell!

8. Add a dash of fun.

Running around like a headless chicken doesn't serve any pur-
pose, other than making you feel like, well, a headless chicken.
Besides, there must be a better way of preparing for the holidays.
How about trying to actually enjoy them for a change?

Of course, putting your feet up and enjoying the sleigh ride is
easier said than done, especially when your to-do list rivals

Santa's. There is a way to add some joy: Try to enjoy the process of holiday prep.

For instance, instead of robotically plowing through your holiday card list, put on some festive music, grab a hot toddy, and get to work. Before you know it, your list will be complete and you will have actually enjoyed the process. What a concept!

9. Just say no to stress!

"No" is by far the smallest but most difficult-to-utter word in the English language. Why? Because, like Scrooge at Christmas, it makes us appear unkind, ungiving, unhelpful, and self-centered.

Unless you decide to carry the entire holiday burden on your shoulders, you might want to revamp your thinking and just say no from time to time. Instead of perceiving "no" as something evil or negative, see it as an opportunity to be good to yourself. Having a ready-made answer available, so you won't automatically say yes, is key.

For instance, the next time you're asked to bake five dozen Christmas cookies for your church or for your kids' school bake sale (and you really don't want to), try something simple but strong, such as, "No. I'm sorry; I can't help you this time." At first the words will feel alien coming out of your mouth, and you might feel guiltier than sin. But after a bit of time and practice, you'll be saying "no" with ease and gratitude.

10. Don't be a Martha!

With so much going on—presents to purchase, gifts to wrap, cards to send, friends and relatives to appease—keeping your head above water can feel like a Herculean task.

One way to handle this stressed-out, overwhelmed feeling is to focus on the big picture and cut yourself some serious slack. For instance, if you need to bake twenty-four snowman cupcakes for your daughter's kindergarten class, don't worry about decorating each one with a perfect little butter cream carrot nose. You're not Martha Stewart! The cupcakes will taste just as yummy without carrot noses, and no one will notice the difference. The less pressure you place on yourself, the more time you will have to stop and smell the roses—or the cupcakes. Also, you can always go and buy those cupcakes, which will save you time and allow you to use the time for something that you really want to do instead. Remember that you do have choices, and it is up to you to make decisions that will allow you to relax and enjoy the holidays.

Must-Know Info

Helping to Remember the Reason for the Season

Pastor Larry L. Thompson,
First Baptist Church of Fort Lauderdale, www.fbcnet.com

J oyeux Noël (2005) is a Christmas movie that tells a true story that demonstrates the power of Christmas. The movie is set in 1914 when our world was at war. World War I was destroying much of Europe, and hundreds of people were dying every day. Suddenly, on Christmas Eve of that year, something amazing happened; the Germans ceased fire, hung candles on trees, and sang German Christmas carols. The Scottish and French troops responded with their own songs instead of with shells. For that one night and the following day, all the fighting simply stopped. History tells us that the two sides climbed up out of the trenches and huddled together by the fires, exchanging whatever rations they had as gifts.

For one day, the world stopped fighting and enemies remained peaceful throughout the day and into Christmas night. Such peacefulness reflects the true spirit of Christmas. These soldiers had responded to a message of peace that the magnificent angels had dramatically spoken to humble shepherds on the hillsides near Bethlehem long ago. Their proclamation was the birth announcement of Jesus Christ the Savior:

"'Fear not: for behold, I bring you good tidings of great joy, which shall be to all people. For unto you is born this day in the city of David a Savior, which is Christ the Lord. And this shall be a sign unto you; you shall find the baby wrapped in swaddling clothes, lying in a manger.' And suddenly there was with the angel a multitude of the heavenly host praising God, and saying, 'Glory to God in the highest, and on earth peace, good will toward men'" (Luke 2:10–14).

Peace on earth and goodwill to men! How closely have you experienced the angels' message in your Christmas celebrations? How far have you strayed from the original Christmas message? I find it difficult to focus on the peacefulness and goodwill of the season in the frenzy of decorating, shopping, parties, holiday cards, cooking, and the incessant commercialization of Christmas.

According to the Gallup Survey Network, the average American will spend more than $866 on Christmas presents—this number is up more than $200 from ten years ago. This fact reveals a definitive emphasis on spending and can inspire you to think about how to avoid the materialism of Christmas and how to return to the simplicity and peacefulness of the original Christmas.

Recently, I had an interesting conversation with a passenger on a flight home shortly after the previous Christmas season. I sat beside a gentleman who had started life as a coal miner and had eventually purchased his own small coal mine. He explained that he and his wife had to make an intentional decision to show their seven children the real meaning of Christmas. He knew of a family in his community who were in desperate need during the holidays. Coincidentally, this needy family also had seven children. Unfortunately, the father was out of work due to an injury, and the family did not have holiday food or gifts for their children. For this indigent family, Christmas was not about celebrating but about surviving.

On Christmas morning, the wise coal mine owner shared gifts with his children. After his children had opened their gifts, he asked each of them to select his/her favorite gift and to get into the family van so that they could experience the true meaning of Christmas. As he drove his family to the home of this needy family, he told his children about what had happened to them. The coal mine owner also told his children that they would have the choice of either keeping each of their favorite gifts or giving them to the needy children. The wise father then reminded his children that Christmas is all about giving and that God gave the very best gift to the world by sending his Son to be our Savior. What an extraordinary and unforgettable life lesson he gave to his children! What an amazing father; he wisely led his family to understand the real reason for the season.

As I listened to this wonderful story, I was faced with the question, "Have we allowed the commercialization of Christmas to steal the true peace and goodwill of this meaningful holiday?" The commercialization of Christmas has been escalating for years, and Christians, who should celebrate the true meaning of the season, have often been guilty of contributing to the tidal wave of holiday spending and conspicuous consumption. Some reporters at MSNmoney.com have estimated that the cost of the Christmas gifts that are listed in the song "The Twelve Days of Christmas" would cost $78,100 in today's economy!

While this song is not meant to be taken literally, it can be used to represent the new view that most people have of Christmas. Do you continue to focus more and more on the selection and purchasing of gifts rather than the spending of peaceful time with your family and friends? Do you and your family share your goodwill with those who are poor, lonely, or oppressed?

The coal miner from West Virginia motivated me to think of ways to choose peace and goodwill as a family instead of being swept up in the materialism of Christmas. You can help your family and friends concentrate on the real meaning of Christmas by using some of the messages that you hear and see during the season to either affirm the true meaning of the holiday or to expose the lure of commercialization.

You could initiate a family dinner conversation using the song "The Twelve Days of Christmas" and the statistics that I have shared about it above. Ask your family, "What could we do to express our love to our relatives and friends, and even to some strangers, other than spending money on buying gifts?" Allow your own creativity to shine through and discuss some inspirational ideas with your family to bring a new dimension to the holidays.

You can also use some of the great Christmas movies as resources to help your family discuss and refocus their thoughts and actions on the holiday. Movie nights at Christmas could include a simple meal, a movie viewing, and family conversations about each film's message. Here are a few suggestions:

- A *Charlie Brown Christmas*: In this television classic, Charlie Brown wants to put on the world's best Christmas pageant. The message is centered on the fact that the best Christmas pageant will have to include the best-looking props. Were it not for Linus, the entire meaning of the season would have been lost in the preparations!

- *How the Grinch Stole Christmas:* In this film, the big, green, hairy, selfish creature hates people with happy hearts. He thinks that the reason people are joyous at Christmas is because of the gifts that they receive. The Grinch steals all the gifts, decorations, and everything in the town that would even remotely remind people of the Christmas season. What is the real message of this story? The gifts that the Grinch steals in the hopes of ruining the villagers' Christmas do not make him happy, nor do his actions rob the people of their holiday spirit. He discovers that the real joy of Christmas comes from the heart and not from gifts and holiday decorations.

- *Home Alone:* One of my all-time favorite Christmas movies, this story demonstrates the importance of family over anything else—including material possessions.

- *Miracle on 34th Street:* This movie helps us all remember that no matter how old we get, the gift of believing is essential for us to capture the true meaning of Christmas.

- *It's a Wonderful Life:* While this Christmas classic flopped at the box office, it has become one of the all-time holiday classics because of the simple message centered on the influence of one life. Ask your children how the birth of Christ has influenced the world.

You can take some time to provide your family with a less

commercial holiday experience. It is important to think about how you can accomplish this goal. If you discuss and plan your activities early, you will not fall into the same seasonal trap of repeating customs that diminish the real reason for the season. Use these ideas or add some of your own:

1. *Position your Nativity scene as a prominent Christmas decoration.* Children love these decorations, and a child-friendly Nativity scene places the focus on the true message of Christmas. My wife, Cynthia, always gift wraps the Baby Jesus on Christmas Eve, places it under the tree, and makes sure that this is the first gift that is opened on Christmas morning. This gift opening is followed by the reading of the Christmas story, which is found in the Bible in Luke 2:1–20.

2. *Give to others.* Take the time, as a family, to identify someone or some family in your community that is in financial and/or emotional distress and follow the wonderful example of my coal miner friend. Give some nice gifts to those who do not have the ability to give back to you and spend some time with this person or this family, assisting them with errands and chores.

3. *Go caroling with your family and friends.* The singing of Christmas carols celebrates the birth of Christ. You can also arrange to visit a nursing home or a hospital and, if permissible, go caroling in the hallways to cheer up residents and patients.

4. *Attend a Christmas Eve service with your family.* This is an

excellent way to prepare for Christmas morning and to help you and your family establish the central focus of this holiday.

5. *Think globally.* Look for organizations around the world that are dedicated to helping others and give your family or friends gifts that actually give back to others who are truly in need. My daughter was the first to give me a Christmas present from Oxfam International a few years ago. She gave me a card that read: "Dad, 10 chickens have been given in your name to a family in the developing world that really needs them. I pray you have a very Merry Christmas! Love, Taylor."

6. *Remember the true reason we celebrate Christmas.* You can downplay the commercialization of Christmas to your family by using the birth of Christ as an example. Simply let each of your children make a list of three items that he/she would like to receive as Christmas gifts. You can then explain the Christmas story, which centers on how the wise men brought three gifts to honor and worship the Baby Jesus.

You can definitely concentrate on the true essence of the holiday by first recapturing the spirit of Christmas in your own heart. This choice may very well lead to your best Christmas ever!

Talking Turkey Tips:
Everything You Must Know
About This Popular Bird

Mary Clingman, director, Butterball Turkey Talk-Line

As the director of the Butterball Turkey Talk-Line, my staff and I field more than 100,000 turkey-related phone calls each year. First-time cooks and seasoned professionals phone us with a wide range of questions regarding shopping and storing, preparation, food safety, cooking methods, recipes, and even leftovers. I have put together a Turkey 411 list below to help you prepare a delicious turkey for Christmas or any other day of the year.

Turkey 411

The VIBs: Very Important Basics

- Fresh turkeys need no thawing and are ready to cook. You may purchase a frozen turkey weeks in advance of the holiday, but you will need to allow at least one day of thawing, in the refrigerator, for every four pounds of turkey.

- You will need to have 1½ pounds of turkey per guest for generous servings and leftovers—you never want to run out of turkey. Most people purchase 16-pound turkeys.

- Food safety is very important to prevent food-borne illnesses—wash your hands often. You should always keep raw turkey and other foods separated.

- Turkey is a perishable product—you always have to be aware of the temperature. When turkey is refrigerated, it must be kept at 40 degrees. When the turkey is cooking in the oven, it must reach a minimum temperature of 140 degrees within four hours. Once the turkey has reached 140 degrees, it can continue cooking in your oven to the required temperature (see below in the next section).

- You always must cook your turkey in one step—never cook it partially.

- You never want to keep a turkey at an in-between stage or temperature for half of a day. This is dangerous, because bacteria can grow that will make you quite ill. While turkey that sits out for many hours (after you have eaten) may taste fine, don't be fooled. You should get the turkey from cold to hot within four hours (and then back from hot to cold within two hours).

Cooking and Seasoning Details

- If you use an open-pan roasting method, your turkey will be tender, juicy, and golden brown. It is best to cook your turkey in a shallow 2- to 3-inch pan. Pans with deeper sides make it harder to heat the sides of the turkey.

- The skin of the turkey protects the meat from the heat of

the oven so that it will not dry out. For great flavor, you can season the bird by sliding your hands over the skin with herbs (such as fresh sage, marjoram, and tarragon), crushed garlic, lemon zest, orange zest, and/or Dijon mustard. You can also make a paste, using $1/4$ cup of olive oil or $1/2$ stick of butter, along with the herbs that you like best.

- While you may favor basting your turkey, note that most of this liquid will end up in the drippings. Also, each time you open the oven door, you lose heat, which will lengthen the cooking process.

- Make sure that your turkey is off the bottom of the pan. Some pans have shallow racks with holes that allow for more heat to get around the turkey, more caramelization, and better flavor. If your pan does not have a rack, you can place three or four whole (peeled) carrots across the bottom to lift up the turkey. You can also form a large donut shape out of aluminum foil and place this under the turkey as well.

- Preheat your oven to 325 degrees. Plan to roast your 10- to 18-pound turkey for $3–3 1/2$ hours (unstuffed), and $3 3/4–4 1/2$ hours (stuffed); your 18- to 22-pound turkey for $3 1/2–4$ hours (unstuffed) and $4 1/2–5$ hours (stuffed); and your 22- to 24-pound turkey for $4–4 1/2$ hours (unstuffed), and $5–5 1/2$ hours (stuffed). (There is a roasting schedule at www.Butterball. com.)

- When your turkey is about two-thirds done, loosely cover the top of the turkey with a piece of aluminum foil (the size of a piece of typing paper) to slow down the cooking of the breast meat.

- It is safe to stuff the turkey. You should put the stuffing in the turkey cavity, right before you put the turkey in the oven. You should also take the stuffing out of the turkey within two hours after you take the turkey out of the oven.

- It is important to use an oven-safe meat thermometer, because ovens vary. The breast should be cooked to 170 degrees, the thigh should be cooked to 180 degrees, and the stuffing should be cooked to 165 degrees. To ensure a legitimate reading, you should insert the thermometer into the thickest part of the turkey without touching the bone. Check the turkey temperature with the thermometer when you place the foil over the top of the turkey.

Storage Info and Leftover Suggestions

- To ensure wonderful leftovers, remember to carve the turkey and place it in zippered plastic bags in the refrigerator within two hours after you have removed it from the oven. You can also freeze portions of the turkey in special bags that are made for the freezer. You should use refrigerated turkey and side dishes within three days, frozen stuffing within one month, and frozen turkey within two months.

- For some novel leftover dishes, consider making grilled (or toasted) turkey quesadillas with cheese, mangoes, and onions; turkey casserole; turkey pizza with barbeque sauce, onions, mushrooms, and cheese; turkey salad with mayo, apples, celery, and walnuts; and turkey sandwiches on sourdough bread with plenty of your side dishes from Christmas dinner. (Side dishes should also be stored in the appropriate refrigerator- or freezer-appropriate plastic bags and containers.)

Please phone us at the Butterball Turkey Talk-Line at 1-800-BUTTERBALL (288-8372). More than fifty college-educated home economists are available to answer all of your questions during expanded hours from November 3–December 30, 2008. For additional information and for recipes, please visit www. Butterball.com.

A FEW MORE INTERESTING FACTS

- 47 percent of Americans eat turkey at home for Christmas.

- 49 percent of Americans eat turkey at someone else's home for Christmas.

- 2.7 percent of Americans eat at a restaurant for Christmas.

A SENSATIONAL BUT SIMPLE

TURKEY

Roast Turkey with Cranberry Orange Glaze

The Experts at Butterball Turkey

Preheat oven to 325 degrees F.

Combine marmalade, cranberry juice, maple syrup, vinegar, and salt in small heavy saucepan. Bring to a boil on medium heat, stirring frequently. Reduce heat to low. Cook uncovered, stirring frequently for 12–15 minutes or until glaze is reduced to about one cup.

Remove neck and giblets from body and neck cavities of turkey; discard or refrigerate for another use. Drain juices from turkey and dry turkey with paper towels. Turn wings back to hold neck skin against back of turkey.

Place turkey, breast side up, on a flat roasting rack in a shallow pan. Brush turkey lightly with vegetable oil or cooking spray. Roast turkey for two hours and then cover breast and top of drumsticks loosely with foil to prevent overcooking of breast.

Continue roasting turkey for another 45 minutes, remove foil, and brush generously with glaze. Return foil loosely to top of turkey and cook for another 45 minutes, or until meat thermometer reaches 180 degrees F when inserted into the deepest part of the thigh. Brush with remaining glaze. Let turkey stand 15 minutes before carving.

3/4 CUP ORANGE MARMALADE

3/4 CUP FROZEN CRANBERRY JUICE CONCENTRATE, THAWED

3 TABLESPOONS MAPLE OR MAPLE-FLAVORED SYRUP

1 1/2 TABLESPOONS BALSAMIC VINEGAR

1/2 TABLESPOON SALT

1 BUTTERBALL TURKEY, 14–16 POUNDS, THAWED IF FROZEN

COOKING SPRAY OR VEGETABLE OIL, TO BRUSH ON TURKEY

Prep time: 25 minutes
Total Time: 3 hours, 55 minutes

Servings: 12

A Simple But Sinful Stuffing

Jeanne Bice, Ultimate Christmas Author

I n a skillet over medium heat, melt half a stick of butter. Slowly sauté the onions until translucent. Add the sausages and fry until browned. Break the sausages up with a fork and remove from heat.

Preheat oven to 350 degrees F.

Pour the bread cubes into a large roasting pan. Add the chicken stock and milk, and mix until moist. Add the sausages and onions to the mixture. Add the remaining ½ stick of butter, cut into slices. Sprinkle the packet of dry gravy mix on top and bake for one hour. Stir once or twice while baking.

Be sure to check stuffing for moistness; if it is getting dry, add a bit more stock.

This is a delicious stuffing that everyone in your family will look forward to every year.

1 STICK OF BUTTER

1 LARGE ONION, CHOPPED

1 TUBE OF JIMMY DEAN SAUSAGE

1/2 POUND OF ITALIAN SAUSAGE

2 BOXES OF HERBED CROUTONS OR
1 POUND OF STALE BREAD

1 1/2 CUPS CHICKEN STOCK

1 1/2 CUPS MILK

1/2 TEASPOON SALT

1/2 TEASPOON PEPPER

1 PACKAGE OF DRY PORK GRAVY MIX

Servings: 8–10

HANDCRAFTED

GIFTS

Clever Craft Ideas for Grown-Ups

Renate Hering-Shepherd, www.dreamhomedecorating.com

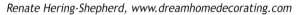

No one else does things quite the same way as *you* do. Even if you do not think of yourself as particularly artistic or "crafty," you can create some homemade gifts that will please your family, friends, and coworkers. Crafting gifts can also be quite relaxing, which is definitely an added bonus. Remember—even a small handmade present shows another person how much you care about him or her. To keep it *really* simple, you could always buy something and then customize it by adding a few personal touches. You never know: your gift might be the one that is treasured for years to come.

Here are some quick and easy ways to create truly "you-nique" Christmas gifts. I hope that you will try creating them. Enjoy yourself and have some fun! It only takes a small personal touch to warm someone's heart with your one-of-a-kind gift.

Gilded Walnuts

Renate Hering-Shepherd, www.dreamhomedecorating.com

Adorning your tree with gilded walnuts is a most historical way of Christmas tree decorating (we're talking sixteenth-century Alsace, Germany, and Switzerland). And that's the beauty of it . . . to *know* that your tree decoration goes back to such an old time and tradition. In wealthy households, the nuts used to be covered in real gold leaf, which reflected both the candlelight and the owners' prosperity, and definitely added to the Christmas splendor. For those who are short on time and technique, you can easily create the same effect of gilding using gold paint. It looks particularly interesting and adds to the rustic charm if you paint only half or three-quarters of the nuts gold and leave the others in their natural colors.

To hang the walnuts:

Cut a tiny notch into the bottom, or crack the two halves open just a fraction at the lower tip, and wedge wire into the notch. Pull the wire up along the "seams" and lock it tight at the top. Finally, create an eyelet by winding a strand of the wire around the end of a pencil or knitting needle. Secure and cut the leftover bits off. Alternatively, just glue a little loop or metal ring to the top of the walnut which works equally well, or you can use a small piece of fabric or yarn to make the loop.

1 PACKAGE OF WHOLE WALNUTS IN THEIR SHELLS

1 TUBE OF PERMANENT GOLD PAINT

1 SMALL PACKAGE OF WIRE, FOR HANGING (AS AN ALTERNATIVE, YOU CAN USE HEAVY-DUTY YARN OR METAL EYELETS)

1 PACKAGE OF RIBBON (SIMPLE RED, RED VELVET, OR RED GINGHAM LOOK NICE)

Frosted Fruit

Renate Hering-Shepherd, www.dreamhomedecorating.com

Frosted fruit decorations make lovely holiday gifts, and they're simple to make.

Select firm, pretty fruits like pomegranates, cherries, and apricots, along with a variety of leaves. Simply brush your selected fruits and leaves with a thin layer of egg white, and then coat each one with granulated sugar. Once dry, place these in a bowl, on a rustic wooden board, or on a plate decorated with a crisp, white doily. It's a fun and festive way to add sparkle and elegance to your home.

Note: To preserve the fruit longer, choose slightly unripe fruit and keep it away from heat sources and in a cool pantry overnight, if possible. If you want to display it for more than a week, choose fruit like apples, cranberries, or clementines.

> VARIETY OF FIRM, SLIGHTLY UNRIPE FRUITS—POMEGRANATES, CHERRIES, AND APRICOTS
>
> VARIETY OF DRIED LEAVES OR STORE-BOUGHT LEAVES
>
> EGG WHITES
>
> GRANULATED SUGAR

Pine Cones That Blush

Collect small or medium-sized fir cones and dry them at home until they are fully opened. Then paint them in deep, glowing colors (different hues of red work really well) and varnish them. They look great when wired in clusters onto the branches of the Christmas tree.

Christmas Rum Balls

Renate Hering-Shepherd, www.dreamhomedecorating.com

I have never met anyone who didn't love my mom's Christmas Rum Balls. In our family, they're the stuff of legend. Everyone used to wait for the first batch to come out of her kitchen on *Nikolaustag* (that's December 6, "Santa Claus Day" in Germany). I'm sure she's now making them in heaven.

Christmas Rum Balls are extremely easy to produce, and they make great last-minute presents. Here's my mom's original recipe. (You'll notice that this is *not* health food. Relax, it's Christmas!)

I POUND CONFECTIONERS' SUGAR, SIFTED

I STICK (4-OZ.) UNSALTED BUTTER

2 HEAPING TABLESPOONS PURE, UNSWEETENED COCOA POWDER (USE ONLY HIGH-QUALITY, FRAGRANT, BITTER-TASTING STUFF; DON'T USE POWDERED, HOT DRINKING CHOCOLATE —IT WON'T WORK!)

2–3 TABLESPOONS RUM

Prep time: 20–40 minutes

Servings: 30 rum balls

$\mathcal{P}$ut all of the ingredients into a mixing bowl and knead the mixture into a brown, gooey mess.

Pinch off pieces the size of small walnuts (or extra-large hazelnuts) and roll into balls.

Coat the rum balls with cocoa powder, chocolate flakes, or toasted, chopped nuts for added flavor.

Leave them to dry for an hour or so and then place these in a cool place in an airtight container.

Ideas for Packaging:

1. Pour into cellophane bags and add lush bows and handmade name tags.

2. Pour them into recycled jelly glasses and cover the lids with circular pieces of pretty fabric. As an alternative to fabric, you could use color photocopies. Think along the lines of copying, for example:

- your favorite striped shirt
- a piece of embroidery
- a photo of something that's perfectly round—say, an antique porcelain plate, a funky brooch, or a flower

Cut out a circle that's 2 inches wider than the lid itself, smooth it over, and tuck it under the lid before screwing it on. Complete the gift with a name tag. Or, instead of a name tag, how about a label for the container? Make it special by handwriting a line from the person's favorite poem or song or a few words that say how much you appreciate having him or her in your life.

MAKING TASTY
MEMORIES

Christmas Memory Tablecloth

Jeanne Bice, Ultimate Christmas Author

I wanted to create a family memento to pass on to my children and their children (I also wanted a way to keep the little ones busy while we were preparing dinner). The answer? A keepsake tablecloth. It's a very simple way to add some holiday fun and create a lasting tradition. You simply find a nice white percale sheet (on sale, of course!) and place it on the table. (Be sure to put down a pad to protect your table.) I usually place two permanent markers on the table—one red and one green—wrapped with red and white gingham ribbon. I put a note around the ribbon that says: Write a holiday message. Draw a picture or write something memorable, then sign your name, along with the year. Kids can draw or trace their handprints and sign their name and age. This is a way to bring out the artist in everyone—guests and new family members included. Everyone adds a new message every year!

After everyone is finished, wash the sheet in cold water and then press it after it dries (pressing it helps set the ink). Truly, it's so much fun to bring out each year and see what we wrote—and what new friends we brought to the table that year.

"Fudging" Your Way to a Great Hostess Gift

Jeanne Bice, Ultimate Christmas Author

With all the hustle and bustle of the holidays, it seems there is always (thankfully!) another party to go to and the annual holiday bake sale to cook for at church or school. Here is my so-simple recipe for fudge that never fails to be well received. To jazz up the presentation, place the fudge in a decorative Christmas tin and finish off with some holiday dishtowels wrapped around it secured with some ribbon or raffia.

Or, for a nice hostess gift, wrap the fudge in cellophane and place it in a gift bag tied with raffia and an ornament for the hostess's tree.

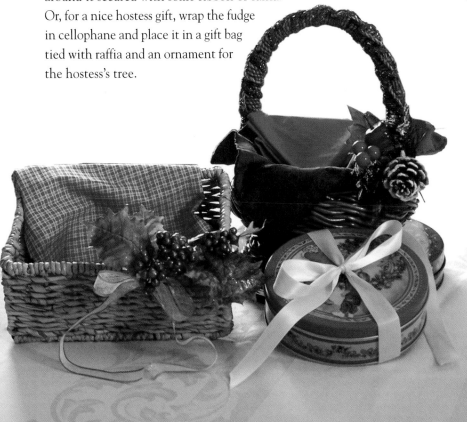

Decadent Christmas Fudge

Combine sugar, butter, salt, and evaporated milk in a saucepan; cook over medium heat until boiling, stirring constantly. Reduce heat to low and cook at a slow boil for 8 minutes without stirring; remove from heat. Add chocolate chips, marshmallows, pecans, and vanilla; stir until marshmallows are melted. Pour mixture into a greased 9 × 9-inch baking pan. Cool and cut into squares.

1 2/3 CUPS SUGAR

2 TABLESPOONS BUTTER

1/2 TEASPOON SALT

2/3 CUP EVAPORATED MILK

1 1/2 CUPS SEMISWEET CHOCOLATE CHIPS

2 1/2 CUPS MINI MARSHMALLOWS

3/4 CUP CHOPPED PECANS

1 1/4 TEASPOONS VANILLA EXTRACT

Makes about 1½ pounds

Must-Know Info

The Dos and Don'ts of the Holiday Newsletter

Ted Pack, Newsletter expert and founder, www.tedpack.org

Holiday letters, or newsletters, are the letters we love to hate. Jason's soccer team led the division. Tiffany played the lead in the school play, made the honor roll again, and was elected homecoming queen. Admit it—sometimes, after dinner, you'll sit around and compare the most elaborate brag letter that you received this year. (My own favorite was from a fellow who wrote that he planned to learn ancient Greek so he could see if the Bible had been translated properly.)

It is hard to avoid bragging in a holiday letter. If Alice made the dean's list and Ralph got off with 150 hours of community service, most people would write about their daughter. Bragging is understandable, but that doesn't mean you should do it.

Here is a list of dos and don'ts for a holiday letter that your friends and family will want to read:

- *Don't brag.* Remember that you may look silly, just like the lady who told us her son was invited to send a biography to "Who's Who in American High School Students." (Main selection criteria: you must order a copy for $49.99.) You may just annoy people with statements that are not especially noteworthy. (If you must brag, see example 3, page 228.)

- *Make it short.* Most people are going to get thirty or forty holiday letters, and they have cookies to bake, presents to buy, and jobs to go to. One thousand words take up about two pages in a 10-point font—that's the most that you should write.

- *Make it readable.* Put a blank line between paragraphs and use two columns if you can. Consider using a 12-point font. Make bigger versions, in 16- or even 24-point font, for your friends and relatives who need larger print. (My standard holiday letters are all about 750 words, with two columns of 12-point font on legal-sized paper.)

- *Keep it light—the holidays are supposed to be happy.* Concentrate on the good things that happened to you and your family over the course of the last year. There are exceptions to this rule. The year that my grandparents died, I mentioned it in my letter, but I wrote about some fond memories we shared (not about the last stages of cancer). Try to avoid writing about illness, infection, and injury.

- *Don't try to get a whole year of memories, accomplishments, and observations into one page.* Focus on a couple of high points. Vacations are always a great thing to write about, unless you took a first-class cruise around the world—which would be bragging.

- *This is not a marketing tool.* Don't use your letter as a sales pitch or a catalog for a home-based business, even if Mary Kay Cosmetics, Amway, or Septic Tank Plus *has* changed your life.

All right, if you can't brag about the kids, and you can't write about your Amway products, what *can* you write about? Here are some suggestions to fill up those two columns:

- You should mention births, deaths, marriages, and moves, so that the old college roommate (who finally makes it out to your part of the country for a visit) knows your wife's name and how many kids you have. Summarize your children for people who haven't heard from you since last year. Mention their ages, heights, and what grades they are in school. If you write "John is a senior this year and set to graduate in June," the graduation announcements he sends out in May won't come as such a shock to people who last saw him when he was twelve. Throw in a picture of the family, too—a picture really is worth a thousand words.

- What is the best book you've read all year? Some of the people you write to may share your interest in murder mysteries, armchair travelogues, or books to read to the kids.

Speaking of reading, the easiest way to improve your own writing is to read good writers. There are lots of people writing short, light pieces today. Dave Barry, Garrison Keillor, Roy Blount, Jr., and Tim Cahill are four of my favorites. Make a trip to your library or used bookstore in October and spend a couple of evenings reading instead of watching television. (See example 1, page 227.)

- Cute things the kids have said are always popular—it shows that they are growing and it isn't bragging. (See example 2, page 227.)

- Write about your job, outside interests, or some of your hobbies. Write about something most people don't know about but might find interesting.

  If you live in an unusual place or have an unusual job, write about it. (Make sure that this information would be unusual to most of the people on your list.) If you moved to a cattle ranch in Arizona, while most of the people you send holiday letters to are still accountants and attorneys back home in New York City, a description of how you spent an afternoon mending fences and shooting rattlesnakes would be interesting. If all of your friends are cattle ranchers in Arizona, they'd be bored. Use good judgment.

  If, sadly, you are housebound, the children have moved away, and you haven't read any good books, you still don't have to write about this year's aches and pains. Write about the holidays when you were a child, or how you met your spouse, or your funniest date in high school. "Not much happened this year. Christmas always reminds me of the time during the Great Depression when we made ornaments out of tinfoil. . . ." Your grandchildren will have a glimpse of real history, and your friends will nod in pleasant agreement, remembering their own experiences. Don't try to cram eighty years into one page. Pick an incident or a season and write about it in enough detail that people will know what it was like.

• Know when to quit. If someone doesn't send you a card, letter, or newsletter for three years, stop sending them your holiday greetings. You can tell yourself they are too busy to write, but you are just fooling yourself. They, in turn, will wonder how long it will take you to take the hint. Sometimes it's like driving a dull nail through a thick plank. Reciprocity is important.

Here are three examples for you to read through that have been taken from my letters over the years:

Example 1: Imitate good writers.

[I was reading Dave Barry just before I sat down to compose this paragraph. (Note: Intentional exaggeration is known as hyperbole in the writing trade.)]

Our son will turn twelve soon. His age and shoe size will be the same. People say "*sixth* grade? Size *12*?" Yup. We made the requisite jokes about black Lab puppies with large paws growing into monster dogs, having a wide base in case of high winds, and going to the poorhouse to pay for a spare set of tennis shoes. He took all of them in good humor. The current style in manly footwear (at least in grade school) tends toward beefy uppers and thick, wide soles. Given his size and the current style, what he wears looks like a pair of bumper cars with laces.

Example 2: Cute things the kids say.

[Historical note: this incident predates ATM cards.]

My daughters, aged four and six, two of their friends, and I went to four Chinese restaurants in a row looking for one that would take either a credit card or a check. At the fourth one, I left the kids in the car, dashed in, saw a sign that said "NO CHECKS ACCEPTED," and asked if they would take a credit card. They said they'd take my check if I showed them my credit card.

I went back out, got the kids, and we sat down at a table. My daughter asked how we were going to pay. I said that the man was going to take my check. She asked how he had printed his sign so quickly. I asked which sign. She said, "That one—'No checks, except Ted.'"

Example 3: Acceptable bragging.

[You can get away with bragging, sometimes, if you poke fun at yourself.]

Our daughter graduated summa cum laude from UCLA last June. "Summa cum laude" is a code for "A little louder." UCLA tries to accommodate graduates' parents, especially the older ones. They put the note next to her name in the program, the sound guy turned up the volume when they announced her name, and we were happy that we could hear it clearly.

Must-Know Info

An Etiquette Primer
on Regifting and
the Dreaded Fruitcake

Barbara Benson Wymer, director of Benson Protocol Company

Regift: (*verb*) To give an unwanted gift to someone else; to give as a gift something one previously received as a gift (*Webster's New Millennium Dictionary of English*, preview edition [v 0.9.6]).

Since Jerry Seinfeld first coined the phrase a decade ago on his extremely popular sitcom, *Seinfeld*, regifting has gained in popularity. It has been reported that a majority of people now find regifting perfectly acceptable.

One of the joys of the holiday season is giving gifts, and you may wonder about regifting etiquette. While everyone loves opening a perfectly wrapped package with a shiny bow, sometimes the gift is kind of disappointing. Remember to always thank the giver sincerely, even if you know that the gift is destined for regifting.

To some people, the idea of regifting is tacky and rude, while others think of it as a form of recycling that is practical and thrifty. Others have a special closet with space to store their unwanted presents.

The Emily Post Institute, etiquette expert Leticia Baldrige, and syndicated columnist Miss Manners all give conditional blessings to the practice of regifting, if you follow the rules. Regifting is a great way to pass along an unwanted gift without the hassle of returning it to the store. Keeping these regifting etiquette tips in mind, you will be able to regift with a guilt-free conscience.

Regifting Etiquette

- Never accidentally regift something to the person who initially gave it to you. Do keep all items that you plan to regift in one place. Write the name of the person who gave you the gift and the date that you received it, so you don't end up giving the present back to the original giver.

- Make sure whomever you regift to does not know the original gift giver. Always regift to people in different social circles.

- Only regift an item if it is in perfect condition. Don't give items you have owned for a long time. A general rule of thumb: if you have to dust it off, it is not eligible for regifting.

- Never regift handmade or one-of-a-kind items. Signed books and monogrammed items are off-limits. Do you have to be told not to regift free promotional items? Some gifts that are good candidates for regifting include good (unopened!) bottles of wine, new household items, and inexpensive jewelry.

- Regift an item only if you are sure that the person you are giving it to will appreciate the item—make sure it is a match. Do you have good intentions? Remember, if you feel that an item is undesirable, the recipient probably will too. If you are regifting simply because you ran out of time, gift cards are simple to obtain and are always well received.

- Do get new wrapping paper and ribbons for recycled items. Don't forget to remove the original card and the gift receipt and always check for notes that the gift giver may have slipped in for you.

- Don't tell the person who is receiving the gift that he/she is being regifted.

- Accept the recycled gift. Even if you suspect you are being regifted, don't mention it.

Consider All Your Options

Donate unwanted gifts to a charitable organization. Some gifts are tax-deductible and you do not need to wrap them.

You can keep an unwanted gift. Remember that someone took the time and trouble to choose something special for you.

Regift your gift cards. Thirty percent of people have regifted gift cards or gift certificates. Never give partial or used gift cards. Before you forget or lose the gift card, you can swap it, buy other gift cards, or sell it. For more information, check out the following websites: swapagift.com, leveragecard.com, and plasticjungle.com.

Instead of doing a traditional gift exchange, throw a regifting party. No one spends a dime and everything comes from your closet, drawers, and storage areas. Each guest brings one wrapped regift. The guests draw numbers and the one with the lowest number chooses a gift and opens it. Each person can take the opened gift or select a new gift. After all of the gifts have been opened, the person with the lowest number gets to trade with someone else or keep the gift he or she has chosen, and so on.

Fruitcake Etiquette

While the fruitcake has been around for centuries, this gift gets no respect. The blame for this negative trend was popularized on the old *Tonight Show*. Show host Johnny Carson used to joke that there was just one holiday fruitcake in the world and that it gets passed around from family to family, year after year.

The jokes about this holiday treat are actually the reason this baked item was invented in the first place—the fruitcake has outstanding durability. In Roman times, the soldiers carried fruitcakes with them during their long travels. During the Middle Ages, the Crusaders also brought this hearty treat along on their search for the Holy Grail. Egyptians put the fruit-and-nut bread in the coffins of friends and relatives because they thought it was the only food that could survive the journey into the afterlife.

There are several theories about fruitcake's ties to the holiday season. Historians say that the bread originated in the Holy Land. Some say its popularity began during the holidays in England in the late 1700s when English citizens passed out slices of the "sinfully rich" cake to the poor women who sang Christmas carols in the streets. Immigrants from Germany, England, and the Caribbean brought their own styles of fruitcake to the United States—that's why there are so many different versions around today.

The jokes about fruitcake's staying power are true because fruitcakes can easily last three years if stored and cared for properly. These cakes need to be tightly wrapped, and you need to pour a small quantity of liquor over them every few months to ensure longevity. Despite the jokes, fruitcakes are still popular, and several million are sold to people in every state in America and to people in two hundred countries.

SOME MORE FUN FACTS

- Food and drink are the most likely type of unwanted items to be passed along, accounting for 35 percent of all regifts, versus 23 percent for beauty and bath products and 18 percent for trinkets and collectibles.

- Fruitcakes account for 15 percent of the food and drink items that people regift.

- Women are twice as likely as men to regift, and nearly 70 percent of adults view regifting or reselling as a type of recycling. Try eBay for your unwanted gifts if you want to earn some extra money.

While fruitcakes became available for mail order in the United States in 1913, they are still sent all over the world today. Most American mass-produced fruitcakes are alcohol-free, but traditional recipes are saturated with liqueur or brandy, and they are covered in powdered sugar (all of which prevent mold). Brandy- or wine-soaked linens can be used to wrap the fruitcakes for storage. Some people believe that fruitcakes, like wine, improve with age.

If you don't regift or throw away your holiday fruitcake, you can recycle it as a doorstop, a paper weight, as bookends, or for feeding the birds. Another unique idea is to attend the "Great Fruitcake Toss" event in Manitou Springs, Colorado. This unusual event, which is held on the first Saturday in January, encourages the use of recycled fruitcakes. Last year marked the 13th annual event and more than 500 people attended the festivities. The all-time "Great Fruitcake Toss" record is 1,420 feet, which was set in January 2007 by a group of eight Boeing engineers.

So if you do keep your holiday fruitcake gift, think about the rich slice of history that has been given to you. If you choose to regift or recycle your fruitcake and the family member or friend asks you, "How was the fruitcake?" you can honestly say, "It was delightful, thanks." Nobody will ever know. Seasons Greetings!

Must-Know Info

Christmas Crafts for Kids

Bernadette Dimitrov, author, speaker, and host of
"Conversations with Mrs. Claus" podcast,
www.hohohochristmas.com

Introducing festive holiday crafting traditions will provide you with the opportunity to enjoy quality time and exceptional holiday experiences with your family. Spending time with your children and crafting Christmas ornaments and gifts will also open the door to creativity and engender a sense of pride and joy in your children. Family and friends will cherish the time and effort, which you and your children have spent, making personalized gifts and ornaments for the holidays.

Creating yearly crafting rituals with your children has many benefits. Your children will learn new skills and you will establish wonderful connections by spending time working together. You can create keepsakes from these special times together, by creating a new Christmas ornament for your tree each year. Imagine the memories that you and your children will have—and the stories you can share year after year—of making these ornaments together. Each year, you can place your collection of hand-made ornaments on your Christmas tree. Some of these ornaments will surely become family heirlooms that will be passed down from one generation to the next.

Luckily, you will not need to spend a lot of money to create terrific Christmas crafts and gift. Remember to focus on the fun that you will all have, spending time together and creating a variety of items. This shared quality time will help to buoy your Christmas spirit. While most people will not remember the cost of most of their purchased gifts, they will remember the warm and fun times that they shared together crafting. Purchased gifts can be lovely, but homemade gifts come with priceless benefits.

General Crafting Tips

Choose a few days and set aside two to three hours each day, or as age-appropriate, so that everyone in your family can have uninterrupted time together for a few activities. Agree not to answer phones and turn off the television sets. Instead, put on some festive Christmas music in the background. Make sure that everyone has some old clothes or smocks on, and agree that it's okay to get messy and to have some fun. Also, allow your children to make choices about what kinds of craft projects they would like to try, and give them time to explore on their own. Through crafting, your children can explore their creative sides and refine their problem-solving skills. Make a list and purchase all of the items, which you will need for your selected activities at your local crafts stores. It also helps if you set aside the items, in individually marked boxes and bags, for each craft project. This organization will ensure that your projects get off to a good start.

 See Christmas Star Photo Tree Ornaments on page 252 and Edible Cookie Ornaments on page 254 for some ideas.

Must-Know Info

Delectable Desserts for the Holidays . . . and Beyond

Lori Karmel, owner, We Take The Cake,
www.wetakethecake.com

Sweet endings should be an integral part of any holiday meal. Unfortunately, many people view dessert as an afterthought. To encourage you to make dessert more of a priority, please take a few moments to think about something: What is the last thing that your guests will eat at your Christmas dinner? Dessert! You should always want your guests to leave your meal with a good taste in their mouths—pun intended. So it would be truly worth the effort for you to make some fabulous homemade desserts to complement your wonderful meal.

Unless you are a chef or a pastry chef, please don't worry if your cake doesn't look professional. Remember, homemade desserts should look homemade, or as we like to call it at the shop "gourmet." I would never want a cake leaving my shop looking "commercial." Most of your guests will be enticed by cakes and cupcakes that look like they have received some special touches and were not just mass-produced. So go out of your way to make the frosting look swirly—just like your grandma did. When it comes to decorations, you can garnish the cake with a Christmas-type of flower or just place a few red roses on the top and take some rose petals and place them around the base. Also, spend some time thinking about presentation. It would be great to display a cake on a beautiful cake pedestal—just make sure that it is not overly ornate, since you don't want your cake plate or pedestal to take all of the attention away from your masterpiece. You can arrange cupcakes either on a cake pedestal or stack two pedestals of differing sizes on top of each other (such as a ten-inch pedestal on the bottom, with an eight-inch pedestal on the top) for a centerpiece display of yummy cupcakes.

Always make sure that you will have enough cake and cupcakes for your guests, because people will be asking for seconds and they will also want to take some desserts home with them. Revel in the compliments that you will receive for your scrumptious desserts and enjoy the holidays!

I hope my recipes on pages 256 and 259 will garner some rave review from your guests.

Must-Know Info

Decorating, the Eco-Friendly Way

Shirley Siluk Gregory, journalist

Christmastime can be hard on the wallet, the waistline, and, yes, sometimes even on the nerves, but it doesn't have to be hard on the environment. There are many easy, inexpensive, and creative ways to brighten your home for the holidays without leaving a heavy footprint on the planet.

In general, you can keep your Yuletide decor earth-friendly by aiming for four simple qualities: energy-efficient, reusable, natural, and local. Here are some terrific tips if you would like to have a truly green Christmas:

Christmas Trees

The keyword here is natural, not reusable. Artificial Christmas trees can last for many years, but they're not as eco-friendly as they might seem. Most of these faux trees are made of either polyvinyl chloride (PVC) or molded polyethylene (PE)—or both—which are petroleum-based plastics. PVC and PE trees are also bad for the environment in other ways: they're not biodegradable and they can release cancer-causing chemicals when they're manufactured, or later when they're incinerated. Some artificial trees also contain lead, which poses another health hazard.

Real Christmas trees don't have any of those nasty toxins, but you still will need to choose carefully. Any real tree will have spent its eight to twelve growing years soaking up carbon dioxide and putting out fresh oxygen, but some evergreens are grown more sustainably than others. Your best bet is to buy or cut your own tree at a local farm (which means fewer fuel miles for transport) that doesn't use synthetic agricultural chemicals. You should always be sure to recycle your tree after the holidays: old Christmas trees can find new life as landscaping mulch, fish refuges, or erosion barriers.

Wreaths and Garlands

As with Christmas trees, the best options are natural. Wreaths and garlands that are made with real pine or fir branches offer all the benefits of real trees plus one more: they don't require a whole tree to be cut down. Instead, it takes just a few branches cut from a live tree to make a beautiful and fragrant wreath or garland. Again, you should stick with a local, eco-minded grower if you can, or make your own if you've got a creative knack and the right kind of evergreen (balsam fir has the best fragrance) in your own backyard.

Candles

All those wonderfully scented candles that you see on sale in the Christmas aisles might seem like a bargain, but they actually carry a steep price for the environment. Most commercially sold candles are made with paraffin, which is another petroleum-based material. When burned, paraffin candles create their own kind of fossil fuel pollution, resulting in black soot that's ugly for you to look at and bad for you to breathe.

Luckily, your earth-friendly Christmas does not have to be candle-free. You can opt to purchase candles that are made with soy wax, beeswax, or bayberry wax (made from the berries of the wax myrtle). These candles are cleaner, more natural alternatives that leave much lighter environmental footprints, especially if you can find a local source. You might even want to try your hand at making your own candles—both for your own home and as holiday gifts for others—to help save both the planet and some holiday cash.

Christmas Lights

You know how hot those old-fashioned Christmas tree lights feel after they have been burning for only a few minutes? That's a sign of how energy-inefficient they are. Unfortunately, much of the electricity you're consuming to keep the lights on is being wasted as heat.

Fortunately, Christmas lights have come a long way in recent years, and strings of cooler-burning, energy-efficient, light-emitting diode lights (LEDs) are now both easier to find and more affordable than ever. LED lights consume anywhere from 3 to 33 percent less energy than incandescent bulbs. These lights also waste less heat and last longer than standard lights.

If you're stringing lights outdoors, you've got an even greener alternative: solar-powered Christmas lights. They're not always easy to find in stores, but if you search online, you can find everything from basic strings of sun-powered LEDs to solar-lit snowballs, snowmen, Santas, and more. Be sure to order early, though: because they're not as widely available as regular lights, solar-powered Christmas lights tend to sell out sooner during the preholiday season.

Gift Wrap

There's something a little sad about all those street-side garbage cans overflowing with ripped wrapping paper, tangled ribbons, and crumpled boxes on December 26. All that waste, all that perfectly recyclable material tossed in the trash—but it doesn't have to be that way.

Your options for kinder, eco-friendlier gift wrap are limited only by your imagination. If you've got the storage space, you can gently iron flat this year's used paper and save it for next year and beyond. Or you can wrap your gifts in brown grocery-bag paper (printed sides in, of course) tied with raffia for a mellow, natural look. You can also cover sturdy boxes and lids in the wrap of your choice to create easy-to-open (and easy-to-reuse) gift packages that don't need tape or ribbon. You can even scout around the local resale shops and flea markets for inexpensive vintage scarves, hatboxes, or baskets that can be just as much of a gift as the items you place inside them.

Finally, here's one more idea for earth-friendly gift wrap that keeps on giving: buy a variety of reusable fabric shopping bags in different colors, patterns, and sizes. That way, everyone on your Christmas list can receive a gift with a bonus: an easy way to decrease the consumption of paper and plastic throughout the year.

Ornaments

Like lights, Christmas ornaments are cheap, plentiful, and tempting to buy during the holiday shopping season. You can trim your tree in a greener way, though, by avoiding the glass and plastic tchotchkes that are shipped from factories located thousands of miles away from your home. Instead, you can look for unique and handmade decorations that are made by craftspeople in your own community. You can even make your own ornaments to add a new look to your holiday tree.

Two of my favorite materials for making handmade ornaments are baking-soda clay and cinnamon dough. The baking-soda clay—made by boiling two parts cornstarch, three parts water, and four parts baking soda—hardens to a beautiful, porcelain-like white finish. The cinnamon dough—a simple mix of nontoxic white glue and cinnamon—stays wonderfully fragrant after it's dry. Look up "cinnamon dough ornaments" on your favorite Internet search engine for recipes and ideas. Both can be rolled, molded, or cut with cookie cutters to create a variety of unique and eco-friendly decorations for your tree—and for your friends' and neighbors' trees, as well.

You shouldn't forget to make popcorn strings—by making and hanging your own garlands of popcorn on trees and shrubs outdoors, you can provide a little holiday spirit for the birds in your neighborhood too.

Fruits, Plants, and More

Depending on where you live, you can find seasonal and festive accents for your home at local farms, farmer's markets, or garden shops. If you live in the northeastern United States, for example, you can decorate your home with bowls of locally grown, cheery, bright-red cranberries. If you reside in Florida, you can buy a bag of Sunshine State–grown oranges, along with some dried cloves, and make your own spicy-scented pomanders.

You can also create a holiday atmosphere in your home with a few glass bowls filled with pinecones, decorative vases filled with walnuts or pecans, a pot or two of heady-scented rosemary trimmed as a Christmas tree topiary, or a few sprigs of holly from your yard (remember to keep the berries away from your children and your pets). If you start with a small garden plant or seeds now, you could have some live and holiday-ready greenery ready to show off to visitors just in time for a visit from St. Nick.

Happy Green Christmas!

Must-Know Info

Spice Up Your Festivities with Pomanders

Cathy Slovensky, advanced master gardener, crafter

Nothing evokes the holidays more vividly than the scent of familiar spices and herbs: a pine wreath on the door, bayberry candles burning on the mantel, and gingerbread cookies baking in the oven. A simple and eco-friendly way to bring the wonderful scent of the holidays into your home is by making clove-studded pomanders. The word "pomander" derives from the French *pomme d'ambre*, which means "ambergris apple." Historically, pomanders were mixtures of ambergris, civet, or musk combined with aromatic herbs and spices and often contained within small gold, silver, and sometimes bejeweled containers that were worn around the neck or waist from a chain or carried in containers called pouncet-boxes. In the sixteenth and seventeenth centuries, people believed that these aromatic mixtures warded off disease, and they were also used to mask odors in unhygienic atmospheres. Early Christians used pomander beads as rosaries, while housewives placed them in cupboards or chests to scent clothes and linens.

Today pomanders are usually made from citrus fruits and spices and used for decorations or for scenting closets and linen chests. Placed in a decorative bowl or basket during the holiday season, pomanders decorated in your own unique style make lovely holiday centerpieces, ornaments, or gifts. One of the most delightful aspects of making pomanders is that it can be a solitary or group project, and even children as young as three can make a pomander with minimal supervision. Put on your favorite holiday music, sip a cup of your favorite beverage, and meditate while you engage in the soothing act of pomander making, or have a pomander party with your friends, neighbors, or family and make it a yearly Christmas event.

SPICE UP YOUR

FESTIVITIES

Making a Pomander

Cathy Slovensky

The amount of spices listed will make enough fixative for several pomanders made with medium-sized oranges. If you are using smaller fruits, you will need less fixative. To make more fixative, just increase the amounts of each spice equally. Adding orris root powder, which is easily found online and at some drugstores or craft stores, will enhance the longevity of your pomander, though it will last a long time even without it.

Mix the ground spices (and orris root powder, if using) together in the Ziploc bag and set aside.

Choose a thin-skinned, unblemished citrus fruit. With the aluminum nail (or your choice of piercing tool), pierce the skin of the fruit in the design that you desire, leaving approximately 1/4 inch or clove head's width between each hole (see Figure 1). If you place them too close together, the skin

Figure 1

will split. The fruit will shrink as it cures, drawing the cloves closer together. Insert the cloves into the pierced holes (see Figure 2).

Figure 2

2 TABLESPOONS GROUND CINNAMON

2 TABLESPOONS GROUND ALLSPICE

2 TABLESPOONS GROUND CLOVES

2 TABLESPOONS GROUND NUTMEG

2 TABLESPOONS ORRIS ROOT POWDER (OPTIONAL; WORKS AS A FIXATIVE)

ZIPLOC BAG (SANDWICH SIZE)

SEVERAL CITRUS FRUITS OF YOUR CHOICE (ORANGE, MANDARIN ORANGE, TANGERINE, LEMON, LIME, KUMQUAT, ETC.)

1/2 TO 1 CUP OF WHOLE CLOVES (DEPENDING ON YOUR DESIGN)

AN ALUMINUM NAIL, KNITTING NEEDLE, OR SKEWER (TO PIERCE THE SKIN OF THE FRUIT)

TISSUE PAPER

When you are finished with your design, place the clove-studded fruit into the spice-filled Ziploc bag and gently shake until the entire piece of fruit is covered. Remove the pomander from the bag, shaking the fixative spices from it (keep any leftover spice mixture for additional fruits). Wrap it in tissue paper and put it in a warm, dark, dry place to cure for two to three weeks. After it has cured, you can remove it from the tissue paper and decorate it or leave it plain. If you've used orris root powder in your spice mix, your pomander will last indefinitely (I have pomanders that are at least twenty years old that I still put out each Christmas).

Design Tips

You can design your pomanders in many different ways. Some people prefer to cover the entire fruit (these stay preserved for the longest amount of time), while others like to experiment with different designs, such as stars, spirals, or horizontal or vertical lines of cloves. You can hang them, using small ones as Christmas tree ornaments (such as kumquats with gold ribbons), or arrange them in a bowl with pinecones, cinnamon sticks, and other holiday decorations. Other ideas:

- You can gild your pomander after it's cured by buying gold craft paint and lightly brushing the clove heads with a brush dipped in the paint.

- Try using two different widths of ribbon for hanging the pomander. For instance, use a dark maroon ribbon as the base ribbon and a thinner pink ribbon on top for a layered effect.

- When giving pomanders as gifts, you can simply wrap them in tissue paper and tie with raffia, or shop at a thrift store for old lace, cotton handkerchiefs, or vintage napkins to wrap them in.

Hanging Pomanders by Ribbons

One of the easiest ways to make a hanging pomander using ribbons is to mark off the orange into vertical quarters with masking tape. Take a length of masking tape that is slightly wider than the width of the ribbon you want to use. Wrap the tape around the fruit from top to bottom. Wrap

another piece of tape around the fruit from top to bottom so that the fruit is divided into quarters (see top and side view in Figure 3).

Figure 3

Use your aluminum nail or piercing tool to puncture the skin of the fruit, filling in each quarter with cloves.

When you have finished filling in each quarter, follow Step 4 from the basic directions above.

After your pomander has cured for several weeks, remove the tape and replace it with ribbon. The easiest way to add the ribbon is to cut two lengths of ribbon the same length, put them together, fold them in half, and tie off a loop at the top (see Figure 4). Then, with the loop at the top, arrange the ribbon where the tape has been removed. After positioning the ribbons on the pomander, tie it off beneath the pomander as snugly as possible. Now it's ready for hanging.

Figure 4

Great Online Resources for Buying Spices in Bulk:

www.frontiercoop.com

www.mountainroseherbs.com

www.thespicehouse.com

KID-FRIENDLY

CRAFTS

Christmas Star Photo Tree Ornaments
(for Three- to Five-Year-Olds)

Bernadette Dimitrov, www.hohohochristmas.com

Place glitter, stars, and sequins into small, individual bowls. Place a pre-cut plain paper star on top of some old newspapers. Take the hole punch and punch one hole at the top of one of the star points (this will be your ribbon goes to hang it).

Place the star on the paper, with the hole at the 12 o'clock point. Put the glass in the center of the star and use the black pen to draw a circle around it. Have your child write his/her name and age in the circle, using the colored pencils or the pen (you can also write it if the child is not able). Then have your child fill in each triangle point around the star with colored pencils.

Spread glue over the edge of the circle and the edges of the star. Have your child sprinkle glitter, stars, or sequins over the glue. Allow these to dry for at least twenty minutes, and then shake off the excess.

Next, turn the star over, ensuring that the hole is still at the 12 o'clock point. Take the glass and place it over the photograph, covering the child's face, and draw with a pen around the edge of the glass. Cut out the face. (If your child is old enough, and confident with scissors, you can allow the child to cut around the circle.)

SILVER, GOLD, AND RED GLITTER, STARS, OR COLORED SEQUINS

LARGE PRE-CUT STARS MADE OUT OF HEAVY CONSTRUCTION PAPER

OLD NEWSPAPER

HOLE PUNCH

ROUND DRINKING GLASS FROM YOUR CUPBOARD

BLACK MARKER PEN

CRAFT GLUE

POM POM BALLS AND/OR GLASS BEADS IN SILVER, GOLD, RED, OR GREEN (OPTIONAL)

RED, GOLD, OR GREEN RIBBON

PHOTOS OF EACH CHILD

SCISSORS

COLORED PENCILS

Turn the cut-out photo over and spread glue over the entire back area. You or your child can now place the photo in the center of the star and press down firmly, so that it adheres to the glue. Spread the glue around the edges of the photograph. If any large blobs of glue go onto the picture, quickly wipe them away with a cloth. Ask your child to sprinkle glitter or stars over the glue. Allow these areas to dry for at least twenty minutes, and then shake off the excess.

Now, spread glue over the remaining areas, and then sprinkle with different colored glitter or sequins. Allow these areas to dry, and then shake off the excess. If there are any areas, that are bare, just add more glue and then cover them with glitter, stars, or sequins.

After all of the stars have dried, thread some ribbon through the hole and get your child to place the stars on the tree! These also make great gifts for grandparents—especially when they are put in red boxes and tied with gold ribbon!

Edible Cookie Ornaments
(for Three- to Eight-Year-Olds)

Bernadette Dimitrov, www.hohohochristmas.com

You can purchase plain gingerbread cookies from a bakery or a grocery store, or you can make them from scratch. Many recipes are available on the Internet or you can find recipes in most Christmas cook books.

Place the sprinkles and decorative balls into small individual bowls. Give each family member three to four cookies to decorate. Add a few drops of food coloring to the frosting and stir until it reaches the desired colors (be careful to add a drop at a time). Next, have each child spread the colored frosting over the surface of each cookie. Now let the fun begin: Use the assorted silver balls and sprinkles to decorate by placing them on the cookie. Allow the decorations to set on the icing for approximately 10 to 15 minutes.

Once the decorations have dried, shake off any loose bits then place the cookies in clear cellophane pieces; then gather and tie each one at the top, with the ribbon. You can also tie these wrapped cookies onto the Christmas tree and you will have a fun and edible treat for Christmas day. These are also great to give as gifts!

4–6 SMALL BOWLS

1 PACKAGE SLICE N' BAKE GINGERBREAD OR SUGAR COOKIE DOUGH, PREPARED PER PACKAGE DIRECTIONS (YOU CAN ALSO PURCHASE PREMADE COOKIES AT THE STORE OR A BAKERY)

SPRINKLES IN VARIOUS COLORS

SILVER DECORATIVE BALLS (THE EDIBLE VERSION)

1 PACKAGE OF WHITE FROSTING

GREEN AND RED FOOD COLORING

ASSORTED COOKIE CUTTERS (GINGERBREAD SHAPE, HEARTS, OR STARS); ALTERNATIVELY USE THE MOUTH OF A PLASTIC CUP AS A CUTTER

RIBBON; RED, GOLD, OR PLAID

CLEAR CELLOPHANE PIECES, CUT INTO LARGE SQUARES (IF GIVING AS A GIFT)

DELECTABLE

DESSERTS

Pumpkin Cupcakes with Cream Cheese Frosting and Caramel Drizzle

Lori Karmel, We Take the Cake, www.wetakethecake.com

Preheat oven to 325 degrees F. Insert cupcake liners into cupcake pans. Mix sugar, eggs, and oil in a mixer on low speed until well combined. Add in the dry ingredients and blend well. Add the pumpkin and mix all of the ingredients on low speed.

Scoop this mixture into the cupcake liners, filling each about three-quarters full. Bake the cupcakes for 20–25 minutes or until a toothpick inserted comes out clean. Let the cupcakes cool before frosting. Swirl the cream cheese frosting (see recipe to follow) on the cupcakes and then drizzle with caramel.

CUPCAKE LINERS

2 1/2 CUPS GRANULATED SUGAR

5 LARGE EGGS

1 1/4 CUPS VEGETABLE OIL

2 1/2 CUPS ALL-PURPOSE FLOUR

2 1/2 TEASPOONS BAKING SODA

1/2 TEASPOON + 1/8 TEASPOON SALT

2 1/2 TEASPOONS CINNAMON

1/2 TEASPOON + 1/8 TEASPOON ALLSPICE

1 3/4 CUPS (15 OZ.) CANNED PUMPKIN

Cream the butter and the cream cheese. Add the sugar and the vanilla and beat until smooth. Don't overbeat this mixture.

Unwrap the caramel candies, making sure that you remove all of the plastic. Combine the caramels and the milk together in a microwave-safe bowl. Microwave for 1–2 minutes or until they have melted.

CREAM CHEESE FROSTING:

1/4 POUND (1 STICK) UNSALTED BUTTER

3/4 POUND (12 OZ.) CREAM CHEESE

3 3/4 CUPS POWDERED SUGAR

1/4 TEASPOON VANILLA EXTRACT

CARAMEL DRIZZLE:

24 CARAMEL CANDIES

1 TABLESPOON MILK

Servings: 26 cupcakes

Caribbean Christmas Rum Cake with Cream Cheese Frosting

Lori Karmel, We Take the Cake, www.wetakethecake.com

Preheat oven to 325 degrees F.

Thoroughly grease two 9-inch cake pans with cooking spray. Cream butter and sugar together on low speed, add oil, and mix well.

Add eggs and vanilla and mix until all ingredients are well combined. Add the lemon extract and the rum. On low speed, gradually mix in the dry ingredients, alternating with the heavy cream.

Divide the mixture evenly among the greased cake pans. Bake for 35–40 minutes or until you insert a toothpick and it comes out clean.

Make the rum syrup (see the recipe on page 260). Remove the cakes from the oven and let them cool for 15 minutes. With a wooden skewer or a fork, poke 12–15 holes in each warm cake. Pour 3/4 cup of the rum syrup over the top of each cake, reserving the remaining syrup for later. Let the cakes sit for 15 minutes and remove them from the pans. Brush the cake tops with the remaining syrup. Let the cakes cool before frosting them. Then, slice each cake into two, so that you have four layers total. Fill each slice with a thin layer of the cream cheese frosting. Frost the outside with a cake spatula. For swirls on the icing, use the back of a spoon in a circular motion.

1 1/4 CUPS UNSALTED BUTTER, SOFTENED

2 CUPS PLUS 4 TABLESPOONS GRANULATED SUGAR

9 OZ. VEGETABLE OIL

6 EGGS

1 1/2 TEASPOONS VANILLA EXTRACT

2 TEASPOONS LEMON EXTRACT

1/2 CUP PLUS 2 TABLESPOONS DARK RUM

1 1/2 CUPS HEAVY CREAM

4 1/2 CUPS ALL-PURPOSE FLOUR

1 TEASPOON BAKING SODA

3 1/2 TEASPOONS BAKING POWDER

3/4 TEASPOON SALT

Decorate cake with rolled fondant leaves and berries. Rolled fondant is a sugar dough that rolls out like Play-Doh and can be used with cookie cutters to create designs such as the leaves, or rolled into a ball to make the berries. You can color the fondant with food coloring to make your Christmas colors. Fondant can be purchased through cake decorating supply stores or sites like Wilton (www.wilton.com).

To make the syrup, combine all ingredients in a saucepan and bring to a boil over medium heat for 2–3 minutes.

To make the frosting, cream the butter and the cream cheese. Add the sugar and the vanilla extract and beat on medium until smooth. Don't overbeat this mixture. Add rum and incorporate the rum by gently stirring until mixed.

RUM SYRUP:

1 CUP GRANULATED SUGAR

6 OZ UNSALTED BUTTER

6 OZ DARK RUM

6 TABLESPOONS WATER

CREAM CHEESE FROSTING:

1/4 POUND (1 STICK) UNSALTED BUTTER

3/4 POUND (12 OZ) CREAM CHEESE

3 3/4 CUPS POWDERED SUGAR

1/4 TEASPOON VANILLA EXTRACT

1 TABLESPOON DARK RUM

Servings: 10–12 slices

North Pole Peppermint Pie

Jeanne Bice, Ultimate Christmas Author

This is a great dessert for non-chocolate lovers and for anyone who wants a great dessert that's easy to make and won't add to the heat in your kitchen while the turkey is cooking.

Cream the butter and sugar together until they're lightly mixed. Hand-mix the eggs until blended. Add the chocolate squares and the chocolate chips and mix well. Pour the mixture into a graham cracker crust. Refrigerate for three to four hours. Just before you serve it, spread the whipped cream on top and sprinkle with the crushed candy canes.

2/3 CUP BUTTER

I CUP SUGAR

3 EGGS, BEATEN

TWO I-OUNCE SQUARES OF UNSWEETENED CHOCOLATE

1/3 CUP SEMI-SWEET CHOCOLATE CHIPS, MELTED

ONE 9-INCH PREMADE GRAHAM CRACKER CRUST PIE SHELL

I CUP HEAVY CREAM, WHIPPED; OR USE STORE-BOUGHT WHIPPED CREAM

1/3 CUP CRUSHED PEPPERMINT STICKS, CANDIES, OR CANDY CANES

Servings: 8 Slices

Must-Know Info

Parenting Tips to
Survive the Holidays
(and Curb the Gimmees)

Lyn Vinnick Kaller, Ph.D., licensed psychologist

As the holidays approach, it is important to be aware that your children may begin to feel the excitement and joy that Christmas brings. They may laugh more, be more playful, and enjoy singing songs, going shopping, and participating in other fun activities in preparation for the holidays.

Along with their excitement, though, there may be feelings of worry. Your children may think things such as, "Will I get the gift I was wishing for?" "Will my mommy let me stay up late?" "Will I miss my school friends over the holidays?" "Will there be extra rules at Auntie's house on Christmas Eve?" and "Is Santa really a nice jolly fellow, because sometimes he can seem really big and scary?"

Understanding Children's Feelings and Decoding Their Behavior

Your children may also experience feelings of anticipation about many holiday-related things, such as needing to wait for their school vacation and then for Christmas Eve and Christmas Day;

needing to be patient and waiting to see those perfect and beautiful gifts under the tree on Christmas morning, and wondering if they will receive the gifts they have dreamed about and requested.

It is important for you to understand that children are not usually as capable of being aware of their feelings as you may be, nor are many children able to handle strong feelings much of the time. Even wonderful events, like a big holiday, can make their feelings much bigger and more intense than usual.

With this in mind, it is easy to understand why a child's behavior may change as a result. Obviously, anxious, anticipating, and excited children may be louder, more talkative, and more impulsive, or they may also be more withdrawn. Additionally, your children may whine or regress—acting younger than their stated ages —and they may use inappropriate language, interrupt you (and other adults) more often, and have a more difficult time falling asleep and staying asleep. These behaviors are quite the same as the ones that you and your spouse (or your partner) may be exhibiting, and you may be just as excited and anxious. The difference is, your children don't have the skills and the tools needed to decrease their anxieties and "turn down" the intensity of their excitement and their impulsivity.

Understanding and Curbing "The Gimmees"

In addition to heightened emotions, increased stress levels, and the generally busy time that prevails around the holiday, you probably have another situation to contend with. known as "the gimmees." Are the first two words out of their mouths "I want . . . " followed by a never-ending list of gift requests? While your children may be bombarded with advertisements (on television, on the radio, on the computer, and in magazines and newspapers) about toys, sporting goods, and electronics, it is important to manage their wish lists and their desire for material things. Always have them make a gift list, including their favorite choices. (See below.)

While you may want to buy them some things that they truly desire, you also might consider balancing their consumerism with volunteerism and charity donations. You can arrange to take them to a soup kitchen or to another charity-based location to volunteer, or to a children's home or to the children's ward of a hospital, to bring presents to needy and/or sick children. They would be able to experience, first hand, the pleasure of both giving and receiving gifts. Also, it would be worthwhile if you could try to balance their need to have the latest toys, gadgets, and athletic equipment, with the deeper meaning of the holidays. Take some time to speak about the true meaning of Christmas, tell stories from your own holiday memories, share family photographs of Christmases past, or take them with you to a religious service. You can also spend time making gifts (including baked goods, ornaments, and craft projects) for family members and for others (such as some of the children at a shelter, a home, or a hospital).

If you incorporate these different elements, into your holidays, everyone will benefit. Best of all, the holidays will take on new meaning for you and your children.

Top-Ten Tips for Surviving the Holiday Season

There is no single solution or magic trick to address all of the issues—including "the gimmees"—that can come about at

Christmastime. However, with some forethought and planning, you can anticipate, resolve, and prevent some problems from occurring. If you incorporate some of the suggestions and tools in this list, into your life, you may find that you have more time and the energy to enjoy the beautiful holiday season with your children.

1. *Remain Calm.* Use a quiet voice with a neutral tone. Manage your own frustration, anxiety, anger, and stress first, before coming face-to-face with your children.

2. *Intervene Early.* Catch your children getting too wound-up, upset, or frustrated (e.g. about a desired toy) and do something about it in that moment. Talk about it with them, using open-ended questions starting with what, when, where, why, and how, so that a conversation can occur. *Remember that listening to children is one of the most important parenting skills.*

   By taking the time to truly listen, you can often resolve the problem.

3. *Co-Parent When You Can.* Rely on your spouse, your partner, and/or a close friend, for support around the holidays. This may mean that you baby-sit each other's children, that you share advice, and that you reach out to seek solutions. It is important, during the holidays, to enhance your social support from the community.

4. *Avoid Power Struggles* . . . and "the gimmees," with your children, in a toy store. For example, in a toy store, you could just say "Mom will add that to your wish list and we'll

see what Santa brings you," or "You'll get some of your own money for Christmas, from Grandma, and you will be able to get this with your own money." It is important for you to set limits and not to give in to every demand from your children by being firm. But it is equally important to be fair, reasonable, and flexible.

5. *Be Patient.* Remember that your children may not have the same tools, as you do, nor do they understand the pressures that you are experiencing during the holidays.

6. *Keep Directions Short and Simple.* Make one request, at a time, so that your children can hear the directions and complete each task successfully.

7. *Choose Your Battles!* Some things are more important than others. Decide what things really matter and act accordingly.

8. *Look for Chances to Praise and Reward.* Studies show that praise changes the behavior, of children, much more effectively than punishment. As a parent, you can do something simple, such as writing love notes and leaving them on their pillows, or making comments about their helpfulness, or having them help you with holiday preparations . . . You can also compliment your children, and their efforts, in getting something done—whether or not they complete their tasks.

Remember that children yearn for parental attention and praise—these things are truly the most powerful motivators and they cost nothing other than your time and planning ahead.

9. *Follow through on what you say.* Only make promises about

presents, or going somewhere special, if you can keep the promises. That way, your children will trust that you are truthful and their anxiety levels will decrease.

10. *Avoid Lecturing.* Once an adult starts to lecture to a child, about anything at all, the child will almost invariably tune out right away. Therefore, it is better to use ten words, or less, when speaking with your children. It is important that you make yourself clear and that your children will hear and understand the importance of what you are saying.

Resources

All Things Christmas, www.allthingschristmas.com

All things Christmas was officially launched in 2000 with a goal to enhance the Christmas experience by sharing recipes, crafts, shopping bargains, holiday stories, music, and more. You'll find information on a wide variety of Christmas topics ranging from what types of lights are suitable for decorating inside and out to the history of Santa Claus. It is a site born of the love of the Christmas holidays and has developed into one of the largest websites about Christmas on the Internet.

Allrecipes, 3317 Third Avenue South, Ste D, Seattle, WA 98134; (206) 292-3990; www.allrecipes.com

As the fastest growing independent food Internet site, and part of the Reader's Digest Association, Inc. food and entertaining division, Allrecipes provides insights into the kitchens and cooking passions of home cooks everywhere with more than 2,300 recipes for Christmas favorites and ideas for entertaining on their "Holiday's and Events" pages. The world's largest social network of food and entertaining enthusiasts, the site is visited annually by more than 35 million people who share and download recipes, reviews, photos, personal profiles, and meal ideas. For more than ten years, the Seattle-based site has served as a dynamic, indispensible resource for cooks seeking trusted recipes, entertaining ideas, everyday and holiday meal solutions, practical cooking tips, and food advice.

Give-A-Tree™ Greeting Cards—Arbor Day Foundation, 100 Arbor Avenue, Nebraska City, NE 68410; (888) 448-7337; www.arborday.org/shopping/GiveATree

The Arbor Day Foundation envisions a world where trees and forests are abundant, healthy, sustainable, and highly valued by all people. In many innovative ways, the Arbor Day Foundation works to reach and engage millions of people. One of those innovations is the Give-A-Tree greeting card line. Every card you purchase helps in replanting our national forests which provide wood, habitat, clean air, and drinking water for millions of us. Each Give-A-Tree card honors the recipient with a tree planted in a national forest that has been devastated by insects, disease, and wildfires. This is a truly unique way to let someone know you care during Christmas that makes a lasting difference.

Salvation Army, P.O. Box 269, Alexandra, VA 22313; www.salvationarmyusa.org

The miracle of Christmas is repeated over and over again through the joy of caring and sharing. The traditional red kettle is an integral part of the Christmas scene, with millions of dollars donated each year to aid needy families, seniors, and the homeless, in keeping with the spirit of the season. Donations provide Christmas dinners, clothing, and toys for families in need. Financial assistance also helps with basic necessities, along with seasonal aid. The Salvation Army's Angel Tree Program provides new clothing and/or toys for children. A sponsoring company or corporation places a

Christmas tree in a secure, high-pedestrian traffic area or lobby. The tree is decorated with numbered paper angel tags with the first name, age, and gender of a child who will receive the gift. Contributors remove one or more tags from the tree and purchase appropriate gifts for the child or children described on the tags. The toys are delivered to the local Salvation Army unit and later picked up by parents to distribute to the children on Christmas Day.

Trees for Troops—the Christmas SPIRIT Foundation, 16020 Swingley Ridge Road, Ste 300, Chesterfield, MO 63017; www.christmasspiritfoundation.org, www.treesfortroops.org

Say a special thank-you to all of the military men and women and their families who serve our country every day! FedEx Special Delivery, a division of FedEx Corporation, and the Christmas SPIRIT Foundation, the philanthropic branch of the National Christmas Tree Association (NCTA) have conducted the Trees for Troops program since 2005 when 4,300 trees were delivered to troops and military families in the United States and overseas. By 2007 that number had grown to nearly 17,000 trees shipped to more than 37 military bases in the United States and overseas. You can participate in this program by purchasing trees that are for sale at specific national retail locations. In addition to domestic deliveries, an international shipment departs from the FedEx Express hub in Indianapolis, Indiana, in November destined for service members stationed abroad.

The Must-Know Experts

Mary Clingman has been "talking turkey" for twenty-four years and is the Butterball Turkey Talk-Line director. Mary thoroughly enjoys her job, where she has assisted thousands of callers with a wide range of questions about all aspects of preparing and cooking turkey. She has also conducted more than 1,200 regional and national radio and television interviews. Reporters from NBC's *Today Show*, CNN, MSNBC, *USA Today*, FOX News, WGN, and even *David Letterman* have called upon her to provide their viewers with easy turkey preparation tips during the holidays. Mary graduated from Simpson College in Indianola, Iowa, with a bachelor of arts degree in home economics. Before joining the Butterball Turkey Talk-Line, she freelanced at a wide variety of trade shows and test kitchens, worked at a grilling help-line, and helped at the consumer affairs department at ConAgra Foods, where she answered product preparation questions. Mary lives in Glen Ellyn, Illinois, with her husband and she enjoys spending time with her two children and four grandchildren. In the off-season, she enjoys playing tennis, cooking, and playing the piano.

Bernadette Dimitrov (aka Mrs. Claus) is an Australian author, inspirational speaker, and host of "Conversations with Mrs. Claus," a pod-cast show heard in more than 90 countries, at www.TheFamilyYak.com. Inspirational guests from all over the world share tips, tools, and insights for a great life! Mrs. Claus also answers questions, from children and adults from around the globe each week. Bernadette's free Christmas e-zine and books are available at her website, www.HoHoHoChristmas.com, which features many ideas for keeping the spirit of Christmas alive throughout the year through acts of kindness and generosity.

She has written several books, including *The HoHoHo Factor*, which is about fun, whacky, and joyous celebrations around the world; and *Bluey, Santa's New Recruit!*, a fun and magical children's series. She is the co-author of *Simply Christmas*, a book containing recipes and crafts. To get a free, personalized "Secret Elf Certificate," go to www.HoHoHoChristmas.com.

Rick Dungey works as a public relations manager for the National Christmas Tree Association (NCTA) and has answered media and consumer inquiries for the NCTA for more than ten years. Rick implements many of the NCTA consumer promotion programs and serves as media liaison at the national office. He has gotten Real Tree industry spokespeople interviewed on many television shows, including the NBC Nightly News, CNN, CNN Headline News, *Martha Stewart Living*, *Good Morning America*, the *Today Show*, the *Crook & Chase Show*, Home and Garden Television, and others. Rick coordinates the RealTree Media Week and interacts with more than seven hundred news journalists and media professionals each year

A veteran journalist, **Shirley Siluk Gregory** writes about green living, the environment, and sustainability for a variety of publications and websites, including EcoLocalizer.com, Planetsave.com, GreenOptions.com, and Suite101.com's "Green Living" section. A graduate of Northwestern University with a degree in geological sciences, Shirley lives in northwest Florida with her husband, Scott, and son, Noah.

Renate Hering-Shepherd gave up a teaching career in Germany to study textiles at Chelsea College of Art & Design in London, England. She holds a bachelor of arts in design/textile design. Renate runs two websites: www.dreamhomedecorating.com is a mix of visual inspiration and practical, hands-on decorating advice to help people create homes they love, and www.gift-craft-ideas.com is a source of original ideas, downloadable patterns, and instructions for making truly special gifts. Renate lives in London with her husband, Duncan, a mathematician—she thinks that someone in the family should be able to provide a bit of logic.

Dr. Lyn Vinnick Kaller is a licensed psychologist who received her Ph.D. in clinical psychology from Virginia Commonwealth University/Medical College of Virginia, with specialized training in child and family therapy. She has a private practice in Scarsdale, New York, specializing in the treatment of children, teenagers, parents, and families. Prior to her position as a supervising psychologist in child psychiatry at St. Luke's-Roosevelt Hospital Center, Dr. Kaller was the project director and senior psychologist for a federally funded research treatment program at Long Island Jewish Medical Center in New York. This included work with children with severe disruptive behavior disorders, and their parents, as well as developing parent skills training groups and workshops. She coauthored the book *Skillful Parenting: An Interactive Guide to Raising Great Kids*. She is the senior author of several psychotherapy treatment manuals; has coauthored book chapters on adolescent suicide and on various therapeutic interventions with children; and has published numerous articles pertaining to children's social skills and childhood disruptive behavior disorders. Dr. Kaller lectures extensively at local schools and community centers, as well as making guest appearances on television shows. She lives with her husband and their three children in Scarsdale, New York.

Since 2002, entrepreneur **Lori Karmel** has been the owner of We Take the Cake (WTTC), a unique cake boutique in Fort Lauderdale, Florida. Her cakes have been featured on *Oprah*, several shows on the Food Network, and in many local and national publications, including the *Washington Post*, the *Miami Herald*, and *Entrepreneur Magazine*. In 2004, Oprah Winfrey selected We Take the Cake's Key Lime Bundt Cake as one of her "Favorite Things." Lori's delicious and beautiful cakes are sought out by some of the most discriminating customers—including brides—in the United States. We Take the Cake also supplies desserts to many upscale hotels and resorts, and many of WTTC's cakes and cupcakes are also available at Whole Foods Markets in the Florida region. We Take the Cake's Gourmet Bundt Cakes are available through www.wetakethecake.com, www.neimanmarcus.com, and www.normthompson.com. Additional information is available at www.wetakethecake.com.

Ivy Larson is the coauthor of an Amazon.com #1 bestselling health and diet book, *The Gold Coast Cure* (HCI Books, 2005) and the follow-up *Gold Coast Cure's Fitter, Firmer, Faster Program* (HCI Books, 2007), which she cowrote with her husband, Andrew Larson, M.D. Ivy developed and created all of the healthy whole-foods recipes in both books and currently teaches nutritionally oriented cooking classes at Whole Foods Markets and culinary shops, as well as group classes at private homes. She has appeared on numerous national and regional radio and television programs, including several shows on CNN and Lifetime Television, and the *Montel Williams Show*. Her books have been featured in *Time Magazine*, *Woman's Day*, *Woman's World*, *Fitness Magazine*, *Fit Magazine*, *Healthy Living*, *Health & Fitness*, *Let's Live Magazine*, *Life & Style*, *Star Magazine*, *National Enquirer*, and many others. She is currently working as a healthy lifestyle expert, contributing cooking, fitness, and nutrition tips to the nationally broadcast *Balancing Act* talk show on Lifetime Television. Ivy's next book, a whole-foods cookbook, will be published by Gibbs Smith in May 2009. For additional information on Ivy, please visit her website at www.goldcoastcure.com and her blog at www.wholefoodsmom.blogspot.com.

Ted Pack's website, www.tedpack.org, has many examples of holiday newsletters (some his own, some sent in by alert readers), as well as information on crafting a well-written holiday greeting. His website also offers a great deal of information on genealogy and includes his personal essays as well as his Peace Corps stories and photos. Ted graduated from the University of California at Berkeley with a bachelor of arts degree in English, and then spent two years teaching English in Borneo as a Peace Corps volunteer. When he returned to the United States from his Peace Corps stint, he was a teacher for a short time. He then went on to work as a computer programmer for thirty years—a tribute to an education that stressed a general strengthening of the mind over an accumulation of trivial facts. Ted and his lovely wife live in Hughson, California.

Melissa Roske is a New York–based life and personal coach committed to helping her clients achieve their personal and professional goals. Melissa's path to coaching began circuitously. Upon graduation from Skidmore College in 1986, with a bachelor of arts degree in English, Melissa pursued a successful career as a magazine editor and journalist in New York and Europe. Her advice column in *J17* magazine, Britain's leading young women's weekly, quickly earned a loyal following and caught the attention of the British media, including the *Times*, the *Guardian*, the *Daily Mail*, the *Daily Express*, and the BBC. Upon her return to the Big Apple in 1998, Melissa trained as a life coach at New York University and was promptly certified by the International Coach Federation (ICF). Melissa continues to publish internationally and helms a thriving coaching practice, Wheels in Motion Coaching (www.wheelsinmotioncoaching.com), in New York City.

A native Montanan with a B.A. in English literature, **Cathy Slovensky** has worked in the publishing field for more than thirty years, publishing articles on Montana history and subjects ranging from rodeo to religion. She works as a freelance editor and proofreader for several East Coast publishers. She and her husband, Bill, owned and operated Chamomylle Cottage, an herbal products business in Montana, for eight years (with help from their children, Sarah and Will) before moving to beautiful Walla Walla, Washington. Also certified in advanced master gardening, Cathy is currently compiling a book of her original, organic herbal recipes and gifts from the Chamomylle Cottage line. Not just at Christmas, but all the year through, she is most thankful for faithful friends and family, especially Bill, Sarah, and Will and those who have come into her life because of them: Brandon, Jade, Kyler, Jana, and little Tilly—the gifts who keep on giving. Write her at cathy.slovensky.56@gmail.com.

Dr. Larry L. Thompson just completed his fourteenth year as the senior pastor at the 13,000-member First Baptist Church of Fort Lauderdale, Florida. Pastor Thompson's innovative methods feature a team approach to ministry that helps members discover their personal gifts, talents, and passions, thus increasing their effectiveness in helping others. In 2006, Pastor Thompson received the National Conference on Community and Justice's Silver Medallion Award, presented to "individuals who have demonstrated leadership in promoting diversity and inclusiveness." First Baptist Church of Fort Lauderdale (www.fbcnet.com) is a unique entity, having successfully transitioned from a traditional, homogenous congregation to a multicultural community with members from nearly seventy different nations. Weekly services are translated into five languages and transmitted live and on the Internet. The church is also host to the Fort Lauderdale Christmas Pageant, a million-dollar, nationally televised holiday production. More than fifty thousand South Florida residents make one of the pageant's nineteen performances part of their Christmas season. Pastor Thompson wrote *Hidden Heroes*, a book about unsung biblical characters who achieved extraordinary accomplishments. He developed the Watchman Prayer Ministry, an intercessory prayer program used in more than two thousand churches. Pastor Thompson also developed the POP Strategy for outreach and wrote the accompanying booklet, *The Path*. He received an honorary doctorate of letters from the University of Mobile for his efforts on behalf of international education and another from the California Graduate School of Theology for his work in church growth. He holds a master's degree from Luther Rice Seminary.

Barbara Benson Wymer is the director of Benson Protocol Company, a Florida-based firm specializing in business and social etiquette for adults and children. Barbara teaches clients how to present themselves with confidence and authority. Prior to launching her own company, Barbara had worked with Florida Power and Light Company (FP&L) for more than twenty-nine years. While she started her tenure at FP&L as a home economist, she also held management positions in sales and marketing and customer service. Barbara was certified by the Protocol School of Washington in Washington, D.C. She attended Michigan State University and went on to the University of Miami where she earned her bachelor of science degree in home economics and marketing. She also earned an M.B.A. degree from Florida Atlantic University. She is a member of American/Florida Family and Consumer Sciences, Consumer Science Business Professionals, the Women's Chamber of Commerce of Palm Beach County, Executive Women of the Palm Beaches, the American Cancer Society's Board of Directors of Palm Beach County, and she was a member of Leadership of Palm Beach County Class of 2001. She also teaches etiquette for the Palm Beach Junior League Cotillion.

The Writers

Nancy Bechtolt wrote a travel column, *Ikimasho* (Let's Go), for an English-language weekly newspaper when she lived in Japan from 1971–76. In addition, she penned monthly editorials for her local Unitarian newsletter.

Kathe Campbell lives on a Montana mountain with her mammoth donkeys, a keeshond, and several kitties. She is a prolific writer on Alzheimer's and her stories are found on many e-zines. Kathe is a contributing author to Chicken Soup books, numerous anthologies, *Rx for Writers*, and medical journals. E-mail: kathe@wildblue.net.

Helen Colella is a freelance writer from Colorado whose work appears in parenting magazines across the country. A Chicken Soup for the Soul contributor, Helen writes educational materials and articles/stories for adults and children. She operates Assist-Write, assistwrite@comcast.net, a home-based business offering writing services to independent publishers.

J. Vincent Dugas is a semiretired businessman, now sorting and assembling hundreds of stories written throughout his lifetime.

Terri Elders prefers books as Christmas gifts and shops for her own underwear and jackets. She lives with husband, Ken Wilson, two dogs, and three cats in the country near Colville, Washington. Write her at telders@hotmail.com.

Peggy Frezon is the winner of *Guideposts* 2004 writer's contest and the Children's Writer 2007 personal story contest. Peggy's publishing credits include *Guideposts*, *Teaching Tolerance*, *Positive Thinking*, *Pockets*, Chicken Soup for the Soul titles, and others. She's currently writing a book about dogs and diets. Visit her blog, The Writer's Dog, at thewritersdog.blogspot.com.

Caroline Grant is senior editor of *Literary Mama*, which features her monthly column, Mama at the Movies. She is coeditor of *Mama, PhD: Women Write about Motherhood and Academic Life* (Rutgers University Press, 2008). Write her at carolinemgrant@gmail.com.

Shirley Siluk Gregory, a veteran journalist, writes about green living, the environment, and sustainability for a variety of publications and websites, including Eco-Localizer.com, Planetsave.com, GreenOptions.com, and Suite101.com's "Green Living" section. A graduate of Northwestern University with a degree in geological sciences, Shirley lives in northwest Florida with her husband, Scott, and son, Noah.

Evan Guilford-Blake is an award-winning writer of plays, fiction, creative nonfiction, and journalism. His plays *True Magic* and *The Firebird* have been published by Playscripts, *Nighthawks* by neoNuma Arts Press, and the text for the picture book *Butterflies* by Unibooks. He and his wife, Roxanna, a jewelry designer and freelance writer, live in the Atlanta area.

Lori Hein is the author of *Ribbons of Highway: A Mother-Child Journey Across America* and a contributor to several Chicken Soup for the Soul titles. Her work has appeared in publications worldwide, including the *Boston Globe* and *Philadelphia Inquirer*. Visit her at LoriHein.com or her world travel blog, RibbonsofHighway.blogspot.com.

Sonja Herbert is the author of an award-winning and as yet unpublished novel about her mother surviving the Holocaust in a circus and other true stories. Sonja presently lives in Germany where she is doing research and getting reacquainted with her mother and siblings. Her website is germanwriter.com.

Renate Hering-Shepherd runs two websites: www.dreamhomedecorating.com is a mix of visual inspiration and practical, hands-on decorating advice to help people create homes they love, and www.gift-craft-ideas.com is a source of original ideas, downloadable patterns, and instructions for making truly special gifts. Renate lives in London with her husband, Duncan, a mathematician—she thinks that someone in the family should be able to provide a bit of logic.

Joseph Hesch is a writer and poet who lives and works where he draws much of his inspiration—his hometown of Albany, New York. His poetry has appeared in *Boston Literary* and *Wanderings* magazine.

Marybeth Hicks is the weekly culture columnist for the *Washington Times* newspaper and the author of *Bringing Up Geeks: How to Protect Your Kid's Childhood in a Grow-Up-Too-Fast World*.

Jeanne Hill, R.N., is the author of three hundred inspirational articles including seven in Chicken Soup books. Her award-winning short stories and articles are often chosen for anthologies. She is a contributing editor to *Guideposts* and has published two books, *Daily Breath* (Word Books) and *Secrets of Prayer Joy* (Judson Press).

Joanne Hirase-Stacey is an attorney living in rural Idaho with her husband and dogs. She has published several short stories and articles, as well as a devotional and poetry. When not working, Joanne finds time to enjoy her favorite things: writing, quilting, running, and biking.

Robert Howe is manager and chief naturalist for a Wyoming guest ranch. He travels to South America's jungles whenever he can to study ethnobotany and live in the rain forest with indigenous friends. He has written numerous articles and two books, *Yours, from Wyoming* and *Tigres of the Night*.

Connie Alexander Huddleston spent twelve years in Panama. She enjoys writing about parenting, prayer, and missions. She and her husband, Harry, are marriage and family counselors in Lawrenceburg, Indiana. She can be reached at chuddles@seidata.com.

Nancy Edwards Johnson writes stories and memoirs about growing up in the Blue Ridge Mountains of Virginia. She is a longtime contributor to area magazines and has written a monthly column for *Latitude* magazine, Winston-Salem, North Carolina, for more than two years. Her e-mail address is nancyedwardsjohnson@yahoo.com.

Lyn Vinnick Kaller, Ph.D., is a licensed psychologist with a private practice specializing in the treatment of children, teenagers, parents, and families. Dr. Kaller is a co-author of the book *Skillful Parenting: An Interactive Guide to Raising Great Kids*. She is the senior author of several psychotherapy treatment manuals; has co-authored book chapters on adolescent suicide and on various therapeutic interventions with children; and has published numerous articles pertaining to children's social skills and childhood disruptive behavior disorders. Dr. Kaller lives with her husband and their three children in Scarsdale, New York.

Lori Karmel is the owner of We Take the Cake (WTTC), a unique cake boutique in Fort Lauderdale, Florida. Her cakes have been featured on *Oprah*, several shows on the Food Network, and in many local and national publications, including the *Washington Post*, the *Miami Herald*, and *Entrepreneur* magazine. In 2004, Oprah Winfrey selected We Take the Cake's Key Lime Bundt Cake as one of her "Favorite Things." We Take the Cake's Gourmet Bundt Cakes are available through www.wetakethecake.com, www.neimanmarcus.com, and www.normthompson.com. Additional information is available at www.wetakethecake.com.

Elisa Korentayer is a singer-songwriter and writer based in New York Mills, Minnesota. She performs under the name Elisa Korenne. Learn more at www.elisakorenne.com.

Robyn Kurth is a freelance writer with over fifteen years of experience writing and producing corporate and industrial videos, and a specialty in "writing for the ear." A native of the Chicago area, she currently resides in Orlando, Florida, with her husband, Greg, and children, Alex and Zell. Ms. Kurth's essays have been published in *Chicken Soup for the Chocolate Lover's Soul* and *Democrat's Soul*. She can be reached at rwordworks@earthlink.net.

Andrea Langworthy writes a column for *Rosemount Town Pages* newspaper and another for *Minnesota Good Age*. She won first place in the 2008 *Chicken Soup for the Divorced Soul* Contest. Her work has appeared in the *Lake Country Journal* and *Minnesota Parent* magazines. She coteaches a workshop at the Minneapolis Loft Literary Center.

Ivy Larson is the coauthor of an Amazon.com #1 bestselling health and diet book, *The Gold Coast Cure* (HCI Books, 2005) and the follow-up *Gold Coast Cure's Fitter, Firmer, Faster Program* (HCI Books, 2007), which she cowrote with her husband, Andrew Larson, M.D. Ivy developed and created all of the healthy whole-foods recipes in both books and currently teaches nutritionally oriented cooking classes at Whole Foods Markets and culinary shops, as well as group classes at private homes. For additional information on Ivy, please visit her website at www.goldcoastcure.com and her blog at www.wholefoodsmom.blogspot.com.

Jaye Lewis is an award-winning inspirational author and a frequent contributor to many popular anthology collections. Jaye lives with her family in the Appalachian Mountains of Virginia. Visit her website at www.entertainingangels.org or sign up for her blog at http://entertainingangelsencouragingwords.blogspot.com. E-mail Jaye at jayelewis@comcast.net

Pat Mendoza is an internationally acclaimed storyteller and author. Prior to his entertainment career, Pat served as a police officer for nearly eight years, including a year and a half as a homicide investigator. He also served in the United States Navy for four years. Write him at patmendoza@aol.com or visit his website at www. patmendoza.com.

Linda O'Connell, a veteran early childhood educator, is a widely published writer who enjoys outdoor activities such as camping and walking on Florida's white sandy beaches where she goes to reenergize after each school year. She and her husband Bill enjoy spending time with their blended family of four children and nine grandchildren. Contact her at billin7@juno.com.

Dorri Olds, a native New Yorker, earned a B.F.A. in 1985 and has been a graphic designer ever since. In 1994, she started her Manhattan-based business, DorriOlds.com. Her short stories have been published in Chicken Soup for the Soul books, *New Woman* magazine, and in the book *At Grandmother's Table*.

Todd Outcalt is the author of seventeen books, including the HCI titles *The Best Things in Life Are Free* and *The Healing Touch*. He lives in Brownsburg, Indiana, with his wife and two children.

Ted Pack's website, www.tedpack.org, has many examples of holiday newsletters (some his own, some sent in by alert readers), as well as information on crafting a well-written holiday greeting. His website also offers a great deal of information on genealogy and includes his personal essays as well as his Peace Corps stories and photos. Ted and his lovely wife live in Hughson, California.

Diane Perrone, with an M.A. in advertising/education, is a mother of seven and Grandma Di to sixteen. She writes between babies from Franklin, Wisconsin. Credits include *Redbook, Exclusively Yours, Girl Talk, Catholic Digest, Family Digest, Marquette University* magazine, *Catholic Herald, Milwaukee Journal, Devotions for Writers*, aviation periodicals, and Chicken Soup books. Contact her at Grandma1Di@aol.com.

Wanda Quist grew up in Oregon, graduated from Brigham Young University, and made a career of raising eight children. She enjoys writing, reading, hiking, sewing, and visiting her family. She and her husband, Robert, live in Colorado. They have seventeen grandchildren with two on the way.

Carol McAdoo Rehme is a widely published author and editor who finds her niche—inspirational writing—is the perfect avenue to share life's lessons. She discovers warmth and unconditional love in her work with the frail elderly. Learn more at www.rehme.com. Contact her by e-mail at carol@rehme.com.

Melissa Roske is a New York–based life and personal coach committed to helping her clients achieve their personal and professional goals. Prior to training as a life coach at New York University, Melissa enjoyed a successful career as a magazine editor and journalist in New York and Europe. Melissa is certified by the International Coach Federation (ICF) and continues to publish internationally. You can learn more about her coaching practice, Wheels in Motion Coaching, by visiting www.wheelsinmotion coaching.com.

Donna Rushneck's romantic and inspirational short stories are published widely by national magazines. She hopes to expand to the science fiction and mystery/thriller markets. With more time now to devote to writing, Donna has started working on her first novel.

Ryma Shohami is a technical writer/editor. She lives in Israel with her husband and two daughters. Check out her new blog Write It Down! at http://rymashohami.wordpress.com. Two websites are under construction: one devoted to technical writing, the other to muffins. She dreams of swimming with dolphins in Hawaii.

Candace Simar is a poet and writer living in Pequot Lakes, Minnesota. Her work has appeared in *Dust and Fire*, *Talking Stick*, *Lake Country Journal*, *Her Voice* magazine, the *Otter Tail Review*, *Spirit-Led Writer*, and many online magazines. Learn more at www.candacesimar.com.

Ted Thompson is a freelance writer and columnist living in northern Arkansas with his wife, Roxanne. A former advertising copyrighter and conceptualizer, Ted's stories, articles, and essays have been published in magazines, story collections, and anthologies. In addition to writing he enjoys motorcycling, houseboating, and gardening. Contact him at tedthompson@alltel.net.

Anne Culbreath Watkins lives in Alabama with her banjo player husband, Allen, a beagle named Darby and two loud parrots. She is the author of *The Conure Handbook* and publishes in magazines, websites, and books, including *Chicken Soup for the Dog Lover's Soul*, *Chicken Soup for the Shopper's Soul*, and *Chicken Soup for the Soul Celebrates Grandmothers*.

John Winsor lives in the mountains north of Cody, Wyoming. He's the author of numerous outdoor relationship adventure magazine stories and the book *Love of the Hunt*, short stories using hunting as a metaphor for the search for the meaning of life. He is finishing a family relationship adventure novel.

Debbi Wise was raised in Memphis and lived ten years in Louisiana. She wrote several one-act plays performed in the New Orleans area, including *Makin' Groceries*, *Breakfast at the Southern Café*, and *Vacation*. She lives in Castle Rock, Colorado, with her husband, daughter, and most loyal fan—a long-haired dachshund.

Barbara Benson Wymer is the director of Benson Protocol Company, a Florida-based firm specializing in business and social etiquette for adults and children. Barbara teaches clients how to present themselves with confidence and authority. She is certified by the Protocol School of Washington in Washington, D.C., has served as a public speaker for more than thirty years, and also teaches etiquette for the Palm Beach Junior League Cotillion.

Carla Zwahlen lives in Wolfeboro, New Hampshire, where she plays keyboard at church and other events and teaches private piano lessons. Her paintings hang in galleries and private collections in the United States and in Europe. Currently, she is working on a nonfiction book project from which *Guideposts* published excerpts.

The Photographers

Kelly Andrews is a self-taught, freelance photographer who focuses on the often-overlooked beauty of New Jersey. She has spent a great deal of time photographing the Jersey Shore, making her way down the coast with the goal of finding and photographing the special things that make each shore town unique. Vivid colors and peaceful scenes dominate her work. Beside the shore, some of Kelly's favorite subjects include barns, rural scenes, gardens, flowers and wildlife–especially birds. People often comment that her photographs look like paintings. Kelly's photos have appeared regularly in magazines, books, posters and calendars. Her fine art prints are available in several New Jersey galleries and many of her images can also be seen on her website, www.thrukellyseyes.com.

An avid gardener, Kelly plans her gardens carefully to attract birds, butterflies and other garden bugs to supply readily available subjects. Kelly lives "down the shore" in Barnegat, New Jersey, with her husband Nigel and her children Rachel and Zachary. They are all very patient with her when she stops the car suddenly to grab a shot of something that catches her eye–at least on most days.

Andrea Perrine Brower was born, raised, and educated in upstate New York. She is a graduate from Mohawk Community College in Utica, New York, and the SUNY at Buffalo. After working for a publishing company in New York for two years, she traveled all over the United States and settled in Florida. Andrea has been a graphic designer and part-time photographer for Health Communications, Inc., for over seventeen years. She lives with her husband Ed and daughter Alivia in Parkland, Florida.

After thirty-four years of teaching and coaching at the middle school level, **Keith Clemens** retired from a career in education. Retirement gave Keith the opportunity to devote more time to his life-long interest in photography. As a former athlete and coach, Keith has taken a special interest in photographing a variety of athletic events. He contributes photos weekly to the Suburban One high school athletic conference website, and has created nearly 100 high school and collegiate action-shot photo collages for the athletes and their families. Keith lives in the Philadelphia suburbs with his wife of thirty-six years. Keith and his wife have two children and a grandson. Keith is also the resident photographer at all family and neighborhood functions.

This is the first photo that Keith has had professionally published. In the future, Keith looks forward to honing his photography skills, while enjoying his interests in photography and sports. Contact him at: **kctwain@verizon.net.**

Renate Hering-Shepherd holds a bachelor of arts in textile design. She runs two web sites, www.dreamhomedecorating.com, a mix of practical, hands-on decorating advice, and www.gift-craft-ideas.com, a source of original ideas and downloadable patterns and instructions.

Patrick Noonan is a self-taught photographer who resides with his family in Massachusetts. Having a combined love for tradition and historic New England inspired him to create the timeless photograph that appeared in this book, which personally conveys the true essence of Christmas at home. At age twelve, he was asked by the principal to be the school photographer. With a shiny new Polaroid Instamatic, his photographic journey began. His experience has evolved greatly over the years with works of scenic landscapes, architecture, and intimate portraits. He is currently focusing on portrait photography with an emphasis on maternity, newborns, children and families. Being able to create photographic art for others to enjoy and keep as priceless memories is not only an honor for him, but a reward beyond measure. To his subjects, he is thankful for allowing me him the opportunity to capture the spirit and simple beauty that embodies all of life. Patrick can be reached at pjnphoto@yahoo.com.

Lawna Patterson Oldfield has been an employee of Health Communications for the past two decades. She has been blessed to work from home for the past fourteen years, while raising her two children, Kylie and Blake. She is an amateur photographer whose love for photos started at a very young age and she rarely leaves home without her camera! She's been married to her best friend and soul mate for seventeen years and loves to spend time with her family at the lake, camping, ATV riding, and sharing fellowship with friends.

Wilco Studios is a full-service family owned business serving South Florida for over thirty years. They are dedicated to producing the finest quality creative images for clients, and their work includes portrait photography, product photography, and special events. Contact Wilco Studios at: www.wilcostudios.com.

Karma Wilson is a *New York Times* bestselling children's book author as well as a self-taught professional photographer. Her focus is rural lifestyle and her favorite subjects are people and animals followed by wildflowers and country scenery. Norman Rockwell is Karma's artistic hero, and she strives to bring elements of his style to her photography. Using natural light to illuminate her subjects gives her work a warm, fresh feel. Karma is currently writing a series of touch and feel board books for children that will be illustrated with her photographs of baby animals.

Karma lives in the wilds of Northwestern Montana where there is never a shortage of beauty to photograph. She lives with her husband, three children, three horses, two dogs and one very spoiled cat. You can see more of Karma's photography at www.karmawilsonphotography.com. To learn more about her children's book writing endeavors visit www.karmawilson.com.

The Author

Jeanne Bice is the creator of Quacker Factory, which specializes in the design and sales of whimsical and embellished woman's fashions. Having become a fixture on television shopping Jeanne's apparel line is a perennial best seller on QVC. She is the author of *Pull Yourself Up By Your Brastraps* and *Jeanne Bice's Quacker Factory Christmas*. Jeanne has appeared on *Good Morning America, The View, The Tony Danza Show, The CBS Early Show*, and has been featured in The *New York Times*, The *Wall Street Journal*, The *Washington Post* and many other publications. She has been called the Queen of the Christmas sweater and with the recent release of her Quacker Factory line of holiday home decorations Jeanne has become a leading designer in all things Christmas. Visit www.quackerfactory.com.

Copyright Credits

(continued from page ii)

Index